Moses

Profile In Effective Spiritual Leadership

James H. Logan, Jr.

Moses:

Profile In Effective Spiritual Leadership

James H. Logan, Jr

Copyright © 2019 Broad Wing Press
Lanham, MD 20706
All rights reserved.
ISBN-10: 1-938373-20-0
ISBN-13: 978-1-938373-20-6

Unless otherwise noted, Scripture is taken from the Holy Bible, New International Version© 1973, 1978, 1984 by International Bible Society. Used by permission of Zondervan Publishing House. All rights reserved.

Printed in the United States of American by KDP
Library of Congress Control Number: 2019934159

©  *Broad Wing Press*

Lanham, MD

Dedication

I gratefully dedicate this book to all of the people who have loved and supported me and my ministry over the years. You have encouraged, cajoled, and prodded me patiently, and sometimes not so patiently, bugged me about completing this work. Your confidence in me spurred me along even when I had none in myself.

This is for you!

Thank you!

Contents

Acknowledgements i

Foreword iii

Preface v

Introduction 1

1. An Unlikely Candidate 5

2. The Making of A Leader 15

3. My Way or God's Way? 29

4. In the Fullness of Time 43

5. Called By God 59

6. Consequences 73

7. In the Hands of A Living God 87

Conclusion 113

About the Author 119

Bibliography 123

Acknowledgments

I could not have embarked on this project had it not been for the family and environment into which I was born and out of which I came. My parents recognized the calling of God on my life from an early age and decided not to encourage or discourage it so that I would never be burdened with the belief that I was doing something to please them. They did, however, protect that anointing, being particular about who spoke into my life and whomever I looked to as a mentor. I praise God that He has preserved them to see the fulfillment of many prayer requests through the various twists and turns of my life.

I am grateful to my children, particularly my daughter Jaime, as well as countless church members and spiritual sons and daughters, along with students, who have been hounding me for years to "write that book!"

Finally, I am grateful to God for bringing a woman into my life that has given me beauty out of the ashes of divorce and encouraged me, like Jonathan's armor bearer, to go and do all that God has put in my heart, promising to be with me all the way. Sybil, I love you and am eternally grateful for your love and support.

Foreword

One of my favorite Bible characters is the man by the name of Moses and over the years of my life and ministry I have come to admire and appreciate him more and more. There are several reasons for my affection for and affinity with Moses and they are what makes my excitement about this book so strong.

I admire Moses because, as an African American, he was often lifted both in song and sermon in the church of my childhood as the liberator of his people, and thus he often served as a model and example of those men, and I would add women, who led what is often referred to as "the modern civil rights movement." In fact, Dr. King, perhaps the best known of those leaders, was often referred to as our "Black Moses." What we saw in Moses was a man called and commissioned by God to lead his people to freedom and we believed that if God did it for them and used Moses, He (God) would do it for us as well.

On another level, as a pastor, I have often looked to Moses for both guidance and encouragement as I seek to lead the people God has placed under my care, and when I see how he handled opposition, resistance, reluctance and recalcitrant behavior I see not only examples but hope as well. In my mind, Moses is a leader of rare and special grace. Finally, on a personal note, I am always moved by the description of Moses as the "meekest man" of his time or any time, and that challenges me to guard my heart and check my spirit lest I become conceited and convinced of my own importance. All of these reasons fuel my excitement that my brother Bishop James Logan has taken to hand and heart the task of writing this powerful book on the leadership, life, style, and example of Moses.

When I was a boy, and someone was a truly great basketball player, it would often be said of them, "game knows game," which means one often recognizes in others what is resident in themselves. Jim Logan is a leader. I have seen him from his pre-teen years lead and I have watched him in school, in church, and, in the academy give leadership at various and varied levels, so I am not surprised that he would be led to write about Moses, the quintessential leader, "game knows game" and leaders know leaders.

In this book, you will meet Moses in new, fresh and exciting ways and you will sense that these words come from a man who has the mind of a scholar, the heart of a shepherd and the hand of a scribe. I am glad my brother has given us this work and allowed thirty plus years of leadership life and lessons to bless us. I know that this book will bless your life, I pray it also changes your life as well.

Bishop Timothy J. Clarke
Senior Pastor,
First Church of God
Columbus, Ohio.

Preface

I was born to preach and teach the Word of God, and to pastor a people. It is something that was so deeply etched upon my spirit that I could not run away from it if I tried, and there were many times I tried. I preached my official first sermon at the tender age of thirteen. Suffice it to say that I had no real idea what that meant. I spent the rest of my youth preparing to take on the mantle of leadership I had always known I would carry, and finally, the day came when I would stand before my first congregation as their installed pastor. I was twenty-five years old, a newly graduated alumnus of Princeton Theological Seminary, in touch with my ethnicity and on top of the world; but, totally unprepared to lead God's people.

I was academically prepared to serve a church. I knew how to study to teach and preach. I knew how to visit people in their various crises. Yet, I was not prepared to deal with their various idiosyncrasies. I had a romanticized view of the church and of her people, and I was excited to finally get the chance to impact the lives of the sheep of this pasture. I thought I was ready until I ran headlong into Myrtle. Myrtle was a retired university English professor who on the first Monday following my first

Sunday as a pastor called me to her home for an audience. It would be the first of regular Monday audiences, but this one set the tone for all those that were to follow. In this first audience, she handed me an index card upon which she had listed all the words she thought I had mispronounced the day before. Now mind you, I concentrated in speech communication while in seminary rather than preaching because of style so, of course, I was more than a little taken back by her critique. As my seminary roommate would often say, this was one of those moments when I was visibly stunned. I did the only thing I felt I could do, I graciously accepted the critique and went on my way not realizing what I had done.

This book is not intended to be about Myrtle, nor is it an instructional guide for how to handle the Myrtle(s) in your life. Rather, it is a book on leadership–specifically leadership in the church among God's people. There is far more to leadership than preaching and teaching. It takes a special person to answer the call of God for ministry. I often tell my students, who believe the professional ministry is the vocation for them, that if they truly believe they have been called, then one of two things must be true: they have either been truly called; or, they have taken leave of their senses. Ministry is not like any other vocation. In fact, I prefer to call it an advocation because often it is the ministry that chooses us, or more accurately, it is the Lord that chooses us. My grandmother used to like to say about the ministry that "some were called, some were sent, and others just went."

Like so many things many will do in their lives, ministry is filled with wonder and mystery, and no matter how much one believes they have learned about it, it is only theory until it is necessary to put it into practice. That was me in a nutshell, a child preacher who had become a man, educated and ready. But was I? I was soon to discover how little I knew and how unprepared I was. Let me tell you if you have not figured it out yet: "People are special, especially 'church people'." Like Moses, I came to a people who were entrenched in a way of living developed over a period of time. For Moses, it was 430 years. In my situation, it was twenty, and despite expressed desires for change when it was at hand, the people still resisted. Moses came to deliver the people, his people, more importantly, God's people from their bondage, but they were not ready to move. This little church wanted to change. It knew it needed to change. The calling committee elected by these same people had a mandate to bring somebody who would facilitate change, but when it was at hand, the people resisted.

It is my hope and prayer that something in these pages will provide some guidance and encouragement as you navigate through the various stages of ministry and faithfully navigate your call. This volume one of an intended trilogy addresses leadership among God's people. This first volume is leadership in Egypt. Volume two will be leadership in the wilderness. Volume three will be leadership in the Promised Land. Each carry with it peculiar styles of leadership to be the most effective, and that, my friends, is my greatest hope about this book, that it leads you into greater dimensions of effectiveness where you are and into the greater of your ministry you have yet to experience

Introduction

Much has been written about leadership and spiritual leadership, and there is significant confusion about the two. Contrary to what many may believe the two are not the same. Secular leadership or leadership in the market place has its principles that do not necessarily translate well into the Church of Jesus Christ. Depending on the books researched one may glean a plethora of characteristics or principles. Most of them have these six in common: honesty and integrity, outstanding self-awareness, vision, courage, communication skills, and team building. These principles are easily ported from the market place to the church, but the emphasis is different.

This book draws on more than thirty-eight years of experience as an inner-city pastor. It is written in a climate where formal education for parish ministry is finally taking seriously the necessity to provide instruction in the area of leadership. Much of that training, such as what leaders like John Maxwell provide, does draw upon pastoral experience and the Word of God and so this book will not necessarily pave new ground. Nonetheless, this book is offered in the hopes that this author's extensive experience will provide some important assistance to any seeking it.

Effective spiritual leadership requires at least four things: unflinching obedience to God, correct timing, clear communication, and a willingness to share the burden of leadership with others. No one can deny the importance of honesty, integrity and the like. They are important regardless of the arena in which they are displayed and practiced, but leadership in the household of faith requires more. First, it requires unflinching obedience to God.

When we look at the life of Moses, we see a model for effective leadership. Moses was like no other fully human leader that has lived. He literally walked and talked with God face to face. Deuteronomy says of his life: "Since then, no prophet has risen in Israel like Moses, whom the Lord knew face to face" (Deuteronomy 34:10). Yet, his humanity is plainly evident. When called to go to the King of Egypt and demand the Israelites freedom, he balked, questioning God and finally protested that God should find another. Still, hesitant though he was, he obeyed God without flinching.

Second, effective spiritual leadership requires correct timing. Moses was trained in the courts of Pharaoh, which could only be considered the best training possible in his day. At the same time, he was nursed by his birth mother, and no doubt understood his biological heritage. At the age of forty, he killed an Egyptian taskmaster, perhaps supposing that he was defending one of his Hebrew relatives, but his timing was 'off.' That his timing was incorrect would be borne out as the story progressed. Moses had the best education one could receive at the time, but he had not been trained and prepared by God for a destiny he knew nothing about. That training could only take place in the university of the desert.

Third, effective spiritual leadership requires clear communication. In the Passover, we are able to see that the communication was clear. People knew to paint their doorposts with the blood of the lamb without which the death angel could not and would not pass over. We also will later see that communication was not so clear in the desert where Moses' own brother, Aaron, listened to the voice of the people and facilitated making the golden calf for them to bow down before and worship in complete contradiction of the instructions he had left for them to follow.

Fourth and last, effective spiritual leadership requires a willingness to share the burden of leadership with others. When Jethro, Zipporah's father, comes visit and return Moses' wife and sons He finds Moses sitting at the entrance of the camp from sun-up to sun-down arbitrating the disputes of the people. Jethro tells Moses that his methodology is ineffective and will only succeed in waring Moses out and frustrating the people. Jethro then suggests a different methodology that will result in greater effectiveness.

The Kingdom of God suffers from a drought of effective spiritual leadership. There are all kinds of leaders, but because many of them tend to run after gimmicks and fads, far too many are ineffective. This author does not claim to be the epitome of effectiveness, on the contrary, a claim to being largely ineffective much of the time would be far closer to the truth. However, the years have afforded me the opportunity to walk through seasons of ineffectiveness (some of which came from immaturity) and effectiveness. The Apostle Paul writes: *"When I was a child, I used to speak like a child, think like a child, reason like a child; when I became a man, I did away with childish things"* (1 Cor 12:11). This is book is written in the great hope that something read in it will contribute to the shifting of seasons from immaturity to maturity, from ineffectiveness to effectiveness, and from effectiveness to greater effectiveness.

Chapter One

An Unlikely Candidate?

Moses was not so different from you and me. He was anything but a perfect man. When God called him, he hesitated but was still obedient. Moses appeared an unlikely candidate for the deliverer of Israel. He was educated in Pharaoh's courts, learning all the wisdom of Egypt. He was a great orator and leader but made a fateful mistake that left him intimidated and fearful, demoralized, no self-confidence, and unable to effectively express himself. His self-image dropped below zero, and he suffered from a serious inferiority complex. He retreated to the wilderness and landed on his feet in Midian where he quietly shepherded sheep and raised his family for forty years.

We can profit from looking at how Moses led in an age when secular principles of leadership have encroached upon the faith community. Consider the circumstances under which Moses was born and driven into the wilderness. Chapter one is set against the backdrop of the latter part of the book of

Genesis and the awesome story of Joseph. God uses Joseph's apparent misfortune – being sold by his brothers into slavery – to dramatically provide for the descendants of Abraham whom he had promised to make into a great nation.

Israel came to Egypt a large family of seventy strong. Lived in the land of Goshen, the best of the land in Egypt, where they could graze their herds and flocks as well as that of the Pharaoh. They were honored guests until a new pharaoh came to power that did not remember or care to remember Joseph and the manner in which he preserved Egypt during the years of famine or the relationship his forefathers had with him. "Now a new king arose over Egypt, who did not know Joseph" (Exodus 1:8). Instead, he was intimidated by their numbers and paranoid about their strength. "Look, he said to his people; the Israelites have become much too numerous for us. Come we must deal shrewdly with them, or they will become more numerous and, if war breaks out, will join our enemies, fight against us and leave the country" (Exodus 1:9, 10). Evidently, the king did not want to live with the Israelites and did not want to live without them either. So the Egyptians enslave the Israelites and begin to oppress them miserably.

The king's plan for handling the Israelites was simple: control them, manage their growth. He would first seek to demoralize the Israelites by imposing hard labor. If he could wear them down physically, they would have no energy to reproduce. Under ordinary circumstances, such a plan should have and would have worked. But these were no ordinary people. They were the people of God living in a land that was not their own, and God had already determined they would become a mighty nation. So a plan that should have worked did not, the harder these Israelite men worked the more children they produced which in turn cause the king's anxiety level to escalate.

Now the king is more than a little anxious. His simple plan had failed, it was time for another tactic. Demoralization did not work so now he attempted "murderous birth control." Calling in the chief midwives, Shiphrah and Puah, the king instructed them to murder, kill outright, all the newborn sons. They were to use their skill and represent to the mothers that their precious baby boys had been born dead. The king's tactic sends shivers up my spine when I note the similarity of this plan to the reality of partial birth abortion in our day. We are appalled at the gall of the Egyptian king in his day, and yet the church has taken a seemingly ambivalent attitude toward abortion in general and partial birth abortion in particular.

The king did not count on the integrity of Shiphrah and Puah. The scriptures tell us that they feared God and let the boys live. They risked their own lives to save these boys, and as a consequence, God honored and blessed them. "So God was kind to the midwives, and the people increased and became more numerous. And because the midwives feared God, He gave them families of their own" (Exodus 1:20, 21).

What a diabolical, demonic plan. The king of Egypt was so paranoid, so intimidated that he was willing to allow girls to live, but boys to die. The enemy of our souls knows that the best way to cut off a people's destiny is to destroy their seed.

Girls possess the womb, but boys carry the seed. Today, we should be concerned with the same strategy with a new twist. Boys, particularly African American boys, are not being killed as they are born, but they are systematically being destroyed through ignorance, neglect and the inadequacy of our educational system.

Note how boys seem to drop off a cliff educationally by the time they reach fourth grade if not before. Look at how quickly boys are prescribed medication to control their aggressive, overly active behavior, simply because teachers do not know how to teach them or handle them. Observe how many boys are having to grow up raised by women, without the influence of a father ending up in jail, training schools or locked into some other counterproductive, self-destructive behavior.

The Egyptian king's plan failed again, and again he was not deterred. Instead, he moved from demoralization to murder to infanticide. It was apparent that he could not stop the boys from being born, but he could ferret them out and kill them by throwing them into the Nile River. But thank God for godly parents that hid Moses for three months and then devised a plan to float him in the Nile so that he would be discovered by the king's own daughter, raised in her father's house, but by his own mother. Thank God for parents like Amram and Jochebed (Exodus 6:20) who had not bowed to the pagan religion of Egypt and saw something special, something worth preserving in their baby boy. Thank God they had the foresight to protect their seed.

Who is protecting our seed today? The diabolical plan of

the prince of the world has succeeded far more than the plan of the Egyptian king did in his day. One look at the African American community is revealing—babies making babies with apparently no end in sight. Where are the Amrams and the Jochebeds who are willing to defy the odds and develop a strategy to protect their children?

This discourse is about leadership. Before we get to Moses himself, there are leadership principles we can glean from the events surrounding his birth. We often think of leadership only in terms of giving direction to massive groups of people, but leadership begins in small cohesive groups like families. I want to suggest some principles from the Scripture we have looked at so far that are, generally, related to leadership, but specifically parental leadership.

Principle One: Parents have the responsibility to discern the dangers in society and take measures to protect their children.

Amram and Jochebed had no trouble discerning the dangers awaiting Moses. The king's henchmen were traveling the streets and back alleys of Goshen listening for the sound of crying babies and if it was a male then in the Nile he went. I cannot imagine the stress of trying to keep a baby quiet. Undoubtedly mothers went to great lengths to keep their babies hidden. One can only surmise what desperate measures would have been employed by fearful parents to accomplish such a feat. Amram and Jochebed hid Moses as long as they could and then devised a plan to salvage his life. Perhaps their planning had taken the three months they had hidden Moses as they brainstormed what to do about him.

Moses' parents were proactive. They refused to wait until the king's men discovered Moses, but built an ark out of basket, coated it with tar so that it would float, placed it in the Nile at a time and placed it where the king's daughter would be sure to find it, positioned Miriam in the reeds where she could observe what happened without being discovered and would be able to jump out at the right time. They were ready with a wet nurse, none other than Jochebed, Moses' mother who would ultimately be paid to raise her own son.

Far too many parents are unwilling to exercise parental leadership, either in properly discerning the dangers that await their children or in the setting of boundaries. Too many have acquiesced to the maxim that these are little adults that should not be stifled in their development by the intrusion of their parents. There are too many dangers lurking in the wings ready to devour the unsuspecting child for parents to neglect their leadership responsibility. There are sexual predators out there ready to pounce on our children. There are mind control instruments readily available to our children that are not being sufficiently monitored. What are your children watching on television? What are they listening to on the radio, across the internet, on that walkman or iPod? What are they reading in that magazine? You are not invading their space by asking questions and looking into corners; you are protecting them.

So much of what is available is drastically contrary to Biblical teaching and standards.

> ***Principle Two:*** *Parents must guard themselves against the influences of the prevailing culture to set positive examples for their children.*

While the majority of the Israelites had begun to compromise their faith, it is apparent from Moses' own life that his parents held on to the faith of Abraham, Isaac, and Jacob. The proof of their faithfulness can be seen in the actions of Moses. Coming upon an Egyptian taskmaster brutalizing one of his countrymen, Moses was incensed. His own sense of justice caused him to commit murder. Where did his sense of justice come from? Where did he get this righteous indignation from? It had to have come from his parents that while he lived and was educated in the house of Pharaoh still were able to influence his life and his choices. Perhaps they had shared their own sense of outrage.

Parents need to realize that much of what we know has been caught rather than taught. If one wants to know why a child behaves the way that they do and says the things that they say look at and listen to the parents. It is sobering to, as a parent, hear things that you have said echoed by your children, or as they get older to hear them remind you of things that you have said or have done that you refuse to allow them to say or to do. The days of saying "do as I say and not as I do" are long over. Such a method has never worked. If we are to set good examples for our children then we must guard our own hearts and minds. The influences of this present world are often times very demonic and the parent that is not vigilant will get caught in its snare. One writer puts it this way:

> We must face reality. If we allow the world's system to press us into its mold as parents, we'll not protect our children from Satan's evil darts. They will become like us. Materialistic attitudes and actions beget materialistic attitudes and actions. Dishonesty begets dishonesty. A lukewarm approach to Christianity begets a lukewarm approach to Christianity – if not outright worldliness. Worst of all, hypocrisy – which our children can discern quickly – begets unbelief and rejection of truth! (Gene Getz, *Moses: Freeing Yourself to Know God*)

Principle Three: *Parents need to take biblical, proactive approaches to protect their children from evil influences.*

As I stated above Moses' parents were proactive. They saw the approaching danger and took measures to protect their child. Looking at them, we learn three things:

First, *parents must trust God to help them be faithful parents.* Parenting is one of the many things that we have not been trained to do. Much of what we know about parenting we received from the examples of parents we had, or we knew. It is not uncommon for the new parent, especially, or for the parent that has become frustrated to bemoan the fact that they lack training and skill, and feel so alone.

God has never expected that parents would have to fulfill this calling alone. Instead, God gave parents everything that is needed to be successful as parents. Remember that the battle is not against that which is visible, but rather it is against the rulers, against the authorities, against the powers of this dark world and against the spiritual forces of evil in the heavenly realms" (Ephesians 6:12). That necessitates, therefore, that we are prepared. So, the Apostle Paul admonishes his readers to put on the full armor of God. The bottom line is that God will help parents be successful as parents, but they must trust Him.

Second, *parents must be courageous!* When you look at Amram and Jochebed, you notice immediately that they were anything but ordinary. They were not the least bit intimidated by Pharaoh or by his plans. There is not much difference between the plans of Pharaoh in his day and the strategies of the devil in this day. Just as Pharaoh sought to kill off the Israelite baby boys, so the devil comes to "kill, steal and destroy" (John 10:10). But there is no reason for us to be afraid. "God has not given us a spirit of fear, but of love, power and a sound mind" (2 Timothy 1:7). We have not been given the mindset of timidity. We are not to be cowards, that is how the devil wants us to be. Instead, we should remember that we have power and authority to win.

Third, *parents must develop strategies to protect their children!*

Just as Amram and Jochebed developed a strategy to protect baby Moses so contemporary parents should come up with their own strategies. Be assured of this: the enemy of your soul has a strategy for you. He has studied you. He knows your likes and your temptations. He is aware of your weaknesses and sets all manner of traps and snares designed to trip you up. If he has so studied you, then clearly you must develop a strategy to protect yourself and your children. There is no time to sit idly by while your children are being devoured. Become proactive and go after the devil.

Principle Four: *All Christian adults should join forces to provide safe, Christ- centered environments for children.*

By virtue of our baptism, we are members of the body of Christ. We have a covenantal relationship with one another. Therefore, our children are children of the covenant. And, by virtue of that covenantal relationship, all adult members become their Godparents. Whether one has children or not, or whether their children are grown and out of the nest or still at home "all believers must be alert to the dangers in our society that are attempting to destroy our children. All believers must guard our hearts so we can become godly models" (Getz, pg. 16). You were never designed to face family crisis alone. As a church family, you have resources to help you navigate the hazardous channels of this thing we call parenting.

Chapter Two

The Making of A Leader

Leaders are not born, they are made. For centuries philosophers were convinced that some people were born to lead while others were born to follow, but good, godly leaders are "made." One would think that Moses was destined to be the savior of the Israelite people, which, of course, he was; however, many factors influenced the process of his becoming a great leader. Anywhere along the way, there were opportunities to become other than what God destined him to be. The life of Moses and the choices he made demonstrate how great a love God has for us, His highest creation, that we should be permitted and encouraged to make choices concerning our lives.

Consider, if you will, the birth of Moses. To say that Moses was born into a troubled time would be one of the greatest understatements ever made. In fact, it could not have been a worse time. He was born into an environment of brutal slavery, an environment of fear and intimidation. His life was at subject to termination because of an edit of a ruthless homicidal maniac. The people were demoralized, hopeless and in despair. The worship of and obedience to the God Abraham, Isaac, and Jacob had been supplanted by Egyptian religion, and nobody looked for anything other than rest from the whips of the taskmasters. Nobody, that is, except for his parents.

Amram and Jochebed, the parents of Moses, were crucial to the evolution of Moses as a leader. When we read the birth narrative in the book of Exodus the focus is primarily on Jochebed, but when we get to the book of Hebrews we read: "By faith Moses' parents hid him for three months after he was born, because they saw no ordinary child, and they were not afraid of the king's edict. (Hebrews 11:23)" Thank God for godly parents who have properly placed their fear and their trust. Rather than fear the Egyptian king, they chose to trust God, and why? Because they saw in this child something special. By special I do not mean what every parent sees in their precious babies, but perhaps they saw that God had a special destiny for this child.

When one considers the circumstances surrounding Moses' birth—the cruel environment into which he was born, the effectiveness of his parents plans to spare his life, and the life of privilege he lived, and it is easy to see how these things blended together to set him apart in a unique way; first among the Egyptians, then among the Israelites. I want to suggest some principles for leadership I think are suggested from the formative days of Moses' life and are instructive for us as we seek to lead in our various spheres of influence.

Principle One*: Godly leaders make full use of the time, talent and treasure that God has given them to bring glory to His name.*

Moses was endowed with great natural and spiritual gifts. "He had outstanding physical assets, unusual intellectual abilities, and exceptional leadership skills. (Getz, pg. 20)" When his parents looked at him, Scripture tells us that they saw that he was "a fine child," (NIV) or "a goodly child. (KJV)" In the book of Acts, Deacon Stephen offering his testimony prior to being stoned says, "he was no ordinary child. (Acts 7:20)" The particular Greek word Stephen used to describe Moses can also be translated as "fair," "beautiful," or "handsome." In other words, the description of Moses' physical appearance offered by his parents went beyond the typical response of parents about their newly born children. Moses was beautiful, in a way that went beyond the physical so that his parents could see a great destiny in store for him.

"Man looks at the outward appearance, but the Lord looks at the heart" (1 Samuel 16:7) is what the Bible tells us, and it is true. God is much more interested in a person's inward qualities, the strength of one's character—one's moral integrity than in their external qualities. The world focuses on external qualities such as appearance. When Ronald Reagan was running for president, for example, many people voted for him not so much because they agreed with his policies but because he "looked" presidential.

When one begins to look at the person's outward

appearance, they inevitably run into conflict. First, looks are deceiving. When I was much younger, there was a common proverb that said "beauty is only skin deep, but ugliness runs to the bone," which we would alter by saying, "ugliness runs to the marrow. Too many people get seduced by appearances. Corporations have made billions marketing the "right" look, the "in" hairstyle, the "with it" clothing. One memorial to their success in this effort is written in the blood of countless numbers of young women bound by anorexia trying to secure the "right" body. Another is the numbers of young people on gurneys in emergency rooms or the morgues having been mugged for their clothing and/or their shoes.

Samuel discovered the folly of looking on the outside when he went to anoint a new king for Israel. Israel had already been the route of living with a stereotypical king who looked the part and had the right appearance. Yet, Saul turned out to be a great disappointment and had been repudiated by God. Now Samuel is standing in the house of Jesse, preparing to anoint one of his sons. But none of those paraded before him was the one God had set aside, though they looked the part. Instead, it was David, the one the Bible says was " ruddy, with a fine appearance, and handsome features. (1 Samuel 16:12)"

Even Samuel was fooled. When he looked at Jesse's eldest son, Eliab, he thought that, clearly, he was the one God had chosen. He looked at all seven of Jesse's older sons and none were the one God was looking for. Even Jesse had his own idea of what made for good leadership material. So he did not include David in the search. But God makes it clear that those whom he calls to do great things are not called in the basis of outward impressiveness, but on the basis of inward character.

Moses was unusual in that he had it all: outward impressiveness and inward character. The Jewish historian, Josephus, picked up this point. He tells us that "as Moses grew to manhood, he had such outstanding physical features that the Egyptians looked for the opportunity to catch a glimpse of him as he walked by or floated down the river on his golden barge. (Getz, pg. 21)"

Moses was also a brilliant scholar. He "was educated in all the wisdom of the Egyptians" (Acts 7:22). Living in the court of the king of Egypt, Moses was a beneficiary of the greatest education the world had to offer at that time.

Ancient Egypt was at the forefront of innovation. Nobody has to this day been able to figure out how the pyramids were built, or how bodies were embalmed. Mysteries abound concerning the mathematical insight, the artistic skill, and the feats of engineering that had to have involved in the achievements of Egyptians of his day. Moses was privy to this knowledge, and also able to teach it to others. Stephen goes on to tells his listeners that Moses "was powerful in speech and action" (Acts 7:22b). Again Josephus helps us to get a grasp of how talented Moses really was.

Josephus gives us additional insight regarding Moses' leadership abilities. When the Ethiopians attacked Egypt and were on the verge of defeating them, the Pharaoh appointed Moses as general over the Egyptian army. Under his dynamic leadership, the Ethiopians were driven back and defeated.

Perhaps this is what the Holy Spirit was referring to when he inspired Stephen to utter that Moses "was powerful in" both "speech and action" (Acts 7:22b). (Getz, 22)

Moses was so well educated that he would have had the equivalent of several PhDs. And that education would serve him well as he led a ragtag team of desert babies through the wilderness for forty years. As leader, we need to use the gifts and talents, the treasures that have been given to us to the fullest so they might bring glory and honor to God. No gifts were intended to be hoarded to ourselves, or used for our delight. entertainment or own enrichment Rather, they are for the "common good."

Principle Two: *Godly leaders have to make tough personal choices.*

There is no getting around it; leaders have to make tough choices and difficult decisions. And the toughest choices are quite often the most personal ones. Do not let anyone fool you; there is a heavy price to be paid by those who would lead the people of God. One should never be envious of a godly leader or desirous of their gifting because they may never know the tremendous price that person pays to operate in that level of anointing.

Moses grew up in the lap of luxury, trained by Egyptian scholar, and fed at the king's table. His destiny was secure. He was the son of the daughter of the king and an heir to the throne. He was a bright star, a favorite of the people. He was wealthy beyond comprehension and was set to inherit the wealth of a nation, and yet he made the choice to leave it behind to identify with a slave nation.

Moses knew his heritage. More than likely he lived in his own home with his biological parents through his preschool years. He knew that he was a Hebrew. When he floated down the Nile on his royal barge or rode through the streets on his royal chariot, he could not help but see the brutality the Egyptian taskmasters inflicted on his Hebrew brothers. How could he trade away his heritage though many others had traded away their faith? The writer of Hebrews says of Moses: "By faith Moses, when he had grown up, refused to be known as the son of Pharaoh's daughter" (Hebrews 11:24).

When you decide to lead there are some difficult decisions and some tough choices you will be called upon to make. Many leaders do not want to make tough personal choices. Far too many want to "have their cake and eat it too." Too many leaders are more interested in personal aggrandizement than in personal integrity. So many are busy touting their own accomplishments and promoting personal agendas.

Godly leaders operate from a different perspective. It is not their agenda they follow but that of their heavenly Father. The people of God cannot be like other peoples. They have been called to a new way of life predicated on a relationship with Jesus Christ. It is a selfless, servant life, dedicated to glorifying and honoring the Lord of our lives. To enter into this life necessitates making tough personal choices. Moses could have easily decided to continue the status quo, and go along with the flow, but he made the tough decision to leave it all behind.

Can you imagine the agony Moses had to have gone through deciding what course of action he would take? What would his foster mother say? Note how offended she would have been. Imagine for a moment her possible responses. Would she have accused Moses of being ungrateful? Would she have wept bitter tears bemoaning what could have been? Would she have been personally devastated by his decision? Would she have tried to talk him out of it? When you consider all the possible scenarios, it is easy to see how people opt out of the tough decisions, but godly leaders have to make the tough personal decisions. Are you the kind of leader who is able to make the tough personal decisions? What decisions are you dodging because they are difficult?

Principle Three: *Godly leaders remember and build upon their personal history.*

For Moses, the tough decision he was called upon to make involved whether to "identify with his own people and experience unusual suffering or to maintain his identity with royalty and experience all the things the world had to offer. To choose to identify with his fellow Israelites would lead to an eternal reward. To choose to remain as an Egyptian leader would only give him earthly benefits. (Getz, 23)"

Not everyone will be faced with this type of decision, but eventually most will, which will, in turn, cause them to come to grips with their identity. They will have to ask, "Who am I?

Where do I come from?" The answers to these questions are found in our individual histories. I am first and foremost a child of God. I have been made to be the head and not the tail, to live at the top and not the bottom (Deuteronomy 28:13). I am "a chosen people, a royal priesthood, a holy nation, a people belonging to God that [I] may declare the praises of Him who called [me] out of darkness into His wonderful light" (1 Peter 2:9).

As so many black Christians are prone to say, my blood runs red because of the blood of Jesus. That is who and whose I am, and yet I cannot escape the fact that I am of African descent. It is jumbled together with European bloodlines, but I am still fundamentally an African American.

As an African American, I have a history, a heritage. That carries implications for my life and witness. I cannot be someone or something that I am not, though I cannot allow others to determine what that means. There are many ways to live out that heritage. Some live it out exclusive of other cultural influences, wearing African garments and sporting African hairstyles I choose to celebrate my heritage differently. My heritage is not a stumbling block; rather it is a stepping stone.

It does not matter to me what one's heritage might be as long as they do not dismiss it as irrelevant and forget it, or they allow it to become all-consuming and thereby limit their options. There is great richness in one's heritage, and while there might be things in one's past that are causes for shame, there is always much to celebrate.

Moses was an Israelite. He was raised as an Egyptian, but he was still an Israelite. There was something in him that could not let go of who he was. Perhaps Moses was aware of what God had planned for his life and for that of his people. Perhaps this awareness motivated him to take matters into his own hands and first, attempt to stop the physical abuse of the Egyptian taskmasters, and second to stop Israelite brothers from abusing one another. Whatever his motivation, it was a calculated move on his part. Stephen tells us (Acts 7:23) that Moses made a decision to visit his countrymen. The sense of the text is that he did so with a purpose. It is possible that he had already decided that it was his destiny to be the deliverer of his people. The problem was, however, he was ahead of God's timing. So when he intervened in the brutality of the Egyptian taskmaster and the next as a peacemaker for his brothers, he was operating in his flesh and not according to the direction of God. "And when he was full forty years old, it came into his heart to visit his brethren the children of Israel" (Acts 7:23).

Now it was good for Moses to remember his heritage and build on it. Many leaders fail miserably in not remembering who and whose they are. Before many are aware, their leadership becomes about them and want they want. Had Moses succeeded in *his* plan, he, no doubt, would have failed as a leader and deliverer of Israel. It was important for Moses to have had the training that he had received. It would come in handy later in his pilgrimage, but he also had to be humbled so that God could use him.

I often wonder what kind of man I would have become had

I not had the experiences that I had growing up. Moses was nurtured in the house of Pharaoh. In many ways, I feel as though that is what my experience has been. I was educated in some of the best schools in this country, worshiped in mostly white congregations, lived a sheltered life. Consequently, I thought that I had it all and knew it all only to discover that there was a lot of education I had yet to receive. That education was in hard knocks and failure that awakened me to who I was and what my purpose was to be. I had nearly forgotten where I had come from and who my people were, but this education reminded me of my heritage and history. I now draw from my understanding of myself, gained through this education, to lead people into new levels of their destiny. Knowing who I am is not a liability; instead, it is an asset.

Principle Four: *Godly leaders see beyond the temporal and the material.*

One area that is problematic for contemporary Christian leaders is the question of spiritual rewards versus earthly rewards. Many are quite willing to trade spiritual rewards for earthly rewards. Temporal and material satisfaction gets many of God's people into trouble. Our society is so geared toward material accumulation that even godly leaders have a hard time getting past it. It is to be expected that secular leaders would be inclined to do that which leads to material wealth, but the influences of our society are so great that even the motivation for much of what happens in ministry is money.

If we learn anything from Moses, it is that money was not a factor. Moses living in the house of the king of Egypt already had access to massive amounts of money. He literally wanted for nothing, and had he remained in the royal household he was set to inherit the wealth of an entire nation. But Moses saw beyond the temporal and the material. He "regarded disgrace for the sake of Christ as of greater value than the treasures of Egypt, because he was looking ahead to his reward" (Hebrews 11:26).

There is a great reward waiting for those who are willing to patiently wait on the Lord. David advised, "wait on the Lord: be of good courage, and He will strengthen thine heart" (Psalm 27:14). Great damage occurs when the people of God get out ahead of God, focusing on material gain rather than spiritual gain.

God is not opposed to His people prospering financially. In fact, it is God's desire that we would succeed and proper, but not according to our personal plan. God has a plan for each of our lives. It is a tailor-made plan. I cannot trade it for another's plan. God has designed it with specifically me in mind. God told Jeremiah, "For I know the plans I have for you, declares the Lord, plans to prosper you and not to harm you, plans to give you hope and a future" (Jeremiah 29:11). That plan is available to us simply by walking in obedience to His will and way.

Moses certainly had an awareness that God was going to do something mighty in his life. Why else would he have allowed that Moses would have survived when so many of his countrymen had their lives cut short as infants? Why else would he have been privileged to sit at the feet of the most learned men in Egypt and discover their secrets? Why else would he have learned the art of warfare? So though he was leaving behind great wealth, and though his decision meant rejection, poverty, and suffering, Moses willingly left it behind because he was able to see beyond the temporal and the material.

> ***Principle Five**: Godly leaders are willing to pay the price to inherit the promises of God.*

I have often said that one has to have taken leave of the senses to aspire to godly leadership, especially in the household of faith. It may appear easy, but there is a great price to be paid if one is going to inherit the promises of God. One does not stumble up and become successful. It takes hard work, long hours, years of struggle, rejection, self-denial, sometimes at the expense of a personal life, friendship, and companionship. But when God has called you to a particular task, no price is too great to pay to inherit the promises of God.

Moses would have to pay a great price. When he discovered that his deeds had been discovered he fled for his life into the wilderness. He lost everything that he had to have to flee from the opulence of his lifestyle into the barrenness of the desert and the shepherding of a flock. Forty years he would spend taking a detour from his destiny until such time as God decided to appear to him in a bush that burned but was not consumed.

Far too few godly leaders seem willing to pay the price necessary to get whatever God has in store for them and the people they lead. Most want it easy and they want it fast. One of the most demeaning things that people say to preachers is how easy they have it, only working one day per week. Most people have no idea of what is required in ministry or the individual price leaders pay to be where they are or have what they have.

It is not uncommon for people to become jealous and envious of another persons' accomplishments and/or possessions. Before coveting what someone else has it would be good to know their testimony. It might well be that after discovering what price they had to pay to have what they have and be what they are, no one else may want it for themselves. Leadership demands an exacting price from those who would make themselves available to lead. The price is so heavy that if not careful one can lose perspective lose their family.

God never requires, however, one's family as the price of anointing. In fact, God desires that leaders be effective at home with their families first before they attempt to lead others.

Chapter Three

My Way Or God's Way

One of the toughest things for the people of God to do is to walk fully in God's will for their lives. Many of us are good at sounding spiritual, but when it is decision time we are more prone to do it our way than God's way. No matter how spiritual we think we are somehow we tend to believe that we know best what we should be doing and where we should be going. The problem is that we are quite often wrong and not only wonder what went wrong but want God to fix it for us.

Moses, at the age of forty, had an understanding that he had been born to be the deliverer of his people. He had been prepared in the house of the Pharaoh all his life for such a leadership role. He believed that he not only had what it would take to lead this people but that he also had a righteous cause. What went wrong? Why did he fail? Rather than walk in God's will for his life, Moses attempted to impose his own will.

God certainly had intended for Moses to lead the Israelite

people. One of the things that I have discovered in my life is that God never does or allow a thing without a purpose. God was not the architect of the tragic events of Moses life, but He was the orchestrator of those events. So clearly God had purposed that Moses would be the deliverer of the Israelites. The calling was right, but the timing and the method were all wrong.

I cannot tell you how many times I have walked in God's will for my life, but have at the same time missed His timing. I also cannot tell you how frequently I have heard the voice of God ringing clearly in my spirit, had the timing right but have used the wrong method to get His will accomplished. There have been a number of times that I have excitedly attempted to put into practice some directive I heard from God, only to fall flat on my face. In tears, I would run to God confused complaining about my failure and protesting that I was only doing what He had told me to do; and God would then patiently say that yes He had given the instruction and yes it was His good pleasure that I should do it, but that He had not meant to do it today. It takes a person who is sensitive to the voice of God to hear and know when the timing and the methodology are perfectly aligned.

It is frustrating to believe that you are in God's will and still experience failure and defeat. So I understand how Moses must have felt after he had given up everything that he had been to lead the Israelite people and then be rejected. I understand why he felt that the only course of action open to him was retreating into the wilderness. For while Moses was well trained and educated in the wisdom of Egypt, there was a course of study that he still had not passed, and the information this course of study offered could only be found in the "school of the wilderness."

Effective leaders are not born, they are made! There is a leader in each of us. It is there because of who we are and whose we are. But that leader has to be nurtured into existence. The word nurture means, "to rear, to educate, to train." For most, this training will be done at home in the company of an accepting, supportive environment. But others, it will only happen in the wilderness.

Anybody that has ever stepped out in front of God in their flesh knows what the school of the wilderness is all about. It is in the wilderness that one is confronted with the reality of their situation and circumstance. In the wilderness is where self-discovery occurs. In the wilderness is where one either dies or lives. As you read these words you might be in the wilderness right now. It is barren there. Nothing much seems to grow there. Everything that can go wrong seems to go wrong there.

It is uncomfortable out in the wilderness; it is unfruitful and unproductive there in the wilderness. Often one feels alone in the wilderness. But it also there in the wilderness where one encounters God. After Elijah had disposed of the 450 priests of Baal at the contest on Mt. Carmel and Queen Jezebel had heard about it, he ran because he knew that her threats were not idle and his life was in grave danger. But while he was alone in the wilderness, he had an encounter with God. Like Elijah, Moses is yet to become the leader that God had predestined him to be; still, we can glean some principles for effective leadership from his experience.

Principle One: *Walking in the Flesh will Land You in the Desert.*

When Moses was rejected by his own people and the king hm to executed him, he ran as far as he could run. He had nowhere to go and no one to whom he could turn, so he ran further and further until he was in the desert. The reason Moses had to run in the first place was that he had been operating in the flesh. Whenever one operates in the flesh they are bound to wind up in a place of barrenness. Consider for a moment the times you have labored in your flesh. What did it get you? Though it may have seemed to work in in the short term; in the long run, what did it get you?

The Bible tells us that "our sin will find us out." In other words, no matter how we try to cover up our messes there will be a day of reckoning. Moses looked around him to make certain that no one was watching when he used his strength to kill the Egyptian taskmaster. He buried him in the sand and went on about his business, only to discover the next day that he had been found out and that the king had issued an all points bulletin for his arrest and execution. Moses had done what he thought was wise and best, but because he operated in his wisdom, his strength, his timing, and his methodology he was found out.

We all can say to ourselves at some point. "If I could go

back and do over some of the stupid things I have done or said. If only I had listened when God was speaking. If only I had waited for God to move. But I was too impatient. I thought I had all the answers, or at least I thought I could "get over." But now I am in trouble looking for some relief in a desert because of my own self-will."

Moses ran because he was in trouble. He ran and ran and ran, but notice where he sits down, by a well. Like Moses, there comes a time when you should get tired of running; when you should get tired of existing in the barrenness of the desert and should be ready to sit down. Moses ran until he was tired of running and sat down, and when he did, there was provision for him—fresh, cool drinking water. Things go so much better when we say with Paul that, "God's strength is made perfect in my weakness," and "I can do all things through Christ who gives me strength." But even when you have messed up and walked in your flesh, when you finally sit down God is there to refresh you so you can get back up and into the will of God for your life.

Principle Two: *Spiritual Ends are Never Achieved By Carnal Means.*

The enemy of our souls loves nothing better than for the people of God to resort to carnal means to accomplish the will of God. Moses felt that he was called to leadership, called to be the deliverer of the Israelite people, and of course, we know that he was. But to resort to using violence to accomplish this end was futile. He thought that he had done a good thing that should have endeared him to the people. Instead, he was seen as a bully striving to get his way by force. I am reminded of the nonviolent approach used in the Civil Rights Movement. Dr. Martin Luther King, Jr., was certainly not the originator of the approach Gandhi used in India long the beginning of that movement, but King understood the value of the approach.

I used to hang prominently in my office a picture of Dr. King standing before a portrait of Gandhi. It hung there so long that it yellowed. Beneath the picture was this quotation:

> The ultimate weakness of violence is that it is a descending spiral, begetting the very thing it seeks to destroy. Instead of diminishing evil, it multiplies it. Through violence, you may murder the liar, but you cannot murder the lie, nor establish the truth. Through violence, you murder the hater, but you do not murder hate. In fact, violence merely increases hate. . . Returning violence for violence multiplies violence, adding deeper darkness to a night already devoid of stars. Darkness cannot drive out darkness; only light can do that. Hate cannot drive out hate: Only love can do that.

Our forebearers lived through the tumultuous years of segregation and the early years of integration and they can tell us, first hand, of the horrors associated with those times. What a blood bath it would have become had those who sought to resolve this dark period of our country's history by violence succeeded. We may not, yet, have come as far as we should or accomplished all that is needed, but we have come a long way. And what we have accomplished came about because of a commitment to take the abuse, refusing to return hatred with hatred or violence with violence.

Moses had not processed his actions in the least. He killed the Egyptian taskmaster on a whim. While he understood that his actions would bring retribution if found out, all he knew was that his countryman was being brutalized and he was in the position to do something about it—and he did!. Far too many of God's people are like Moses, reacting to situations rather than discerning correctly the best course of action and when that happens, more often than we want to admit, carnal means are used to accomplish spiritual ends. Godly leaders, effective leaders know that spiritual ends are never achieved by carnal means.

Principle Three*: Timing is as Important as Action.*

How many times have you done the right thing at the wrong time? Timing is not only as important as action, but it might actually be more important. The Bible asserts that "man plans his way, but God directs his steps." It is easy to get out ahead of God, but one thing I have discovered is that when God is in it, things flow; but when the flesh is in it, things are forced. Moses had his timing all wrong, he forced his way, he jumped too quick, and as a result, everything blew up in his face.

Believe it or not, God knows what we need, when we need it, and how we need it. His thoughts are not our thoughts; his ways are not our ways. It might seem as though God has forgotten about us, or that God is not moving fast enough, but God's timing is perfect. God does not operate according to our time. We operate according to chronos–man's time; but God operates according to kairos. For us, everything must be segmented, programmed, and we expect God to operate in the same manner. We are programmed for instant gratification and when it does not happen the way we think it should we are prone to matters into our own hands. Consider the mess Abraham and Sarah made trying to force God's hand, and Ishmael was born.

There have been so many occasions in my life that called for action, and action is what I took, but the timing was all wrong. That is why we all need discernment or knowledge. "Knowledge tells me what to do; wisdom tells me when to do it and how to carry it out. (Swindoll, pg.57)" It is not an easy process, however. My flesh screams out to take action and does not care about timing. This one offended me, and I don't care who is listening or what I am interrupting, or whom I may damage I am going to speak on it now, but the timing is wrong.

Parents need to learn the value and the importance of timing. Children need to learn the value and the importance of timing. Coworkers, spouses, supervisors, and employees need to learn the value and the importance of timing. One can be as right as they can be and still be wrong. "Moses was too strong. Too educated. Too cultured. Too gifted. Too advantaged. He was straining at the leash and had to learn that waiting – pacing himself – was not a sign of weakness but of strength. (Swindoll, pg. 59)"

Regardless of however long it takes for God's will to be accomplished in your life, God's timing is still perfect. You might be frustrated right now as you read these words because your promised future has yet to materialize, but do not take matters into your own hands. Incredible damage is done when we slip out of the spirit and into the flesh. God is still God. He "is not a man that He should lie or the son of man that he should go back on His Word." If God promised to move in your life that is exactly what he will do.

Principle Four*: Spiritual Leadership is not Self-Assumed, It is God Appointed.*

So much of leadership is assumed in our culture. The prevailing manner in which leadership is determined in the world's economy is based upon presentation and survival. If I want to get ahead in the world it is critical that I have an incredible resumé that says, "this one is perfect for the job." It is so incredible, in fact, that one wonders at the validity of the accomplishments listed in it. I look for opportunities for self-promotion, the ways in which I can exalt myself above others. To use an old euphemism, I learn how to "boggart" my way. But that is not the way it works in the household of faith. "No one from the east or the west or from the desert can exalt a man. But it is God who judges: He brings one down, He exalts another" (Psalm 75:6, 7).

In recent times there have been several high profile

scandals in the athletic arena with division one coaches, as well with candidates running for public office in which individuals were hired and accepted positions of great responsibility based on the information in their resumés. But on closer scrutiny, we discovered that many of the claims made in these were not only misleading but, actually, false. The revelation of these false claims invalidated lucrative job offers and brought great embarrassment to the individuals making them as well as the institutions that hired them prior to thoroughly investigating them.

To suggest that such false claims are not made in the faith community would be naive, for certainly there has been many examples of persons seeking to exalt themselves for personal gain in this arena. A worse problem lies in the heart and mind of a person who thinks that they can adequately handle a job that is bigger than they are because of their natural ability. That is what happened to Moses. He surmised that because he was well educated, well decorated as a military officer, well connected in the king's court, and well thought of by the populace that he was a "natural" as the leader of a rebellion by the Israelite people. But, Moses had yet to learn humility.

In the economy of the Kingdom, spiritual leadership does not come because of natural ability, but rather by supernatural anointing. There is a leader in us all, but leadership in the church looks drastically different than it does in the world. Most of those who become great, effective leaders in the church does so with fear and trembling. They were catapulted into leadership often times in spite of their self-will. A.W.

Tozer says, "A true and safe leader is likely one who has no desire to lead but is forced into a position of leadership by the inward pressure of the Holy Spirit and by the press of the external situation" (Tozer, pg. 459).

If you are setting your heart on becoming a leader of a particular caliber believing that you have it "locked" because of who you are and all you have accomplished, I have news for you; God does not work that way. God uses some of the most unlikely people. People who split infinitives, and speak "ebonics," effectively pastor thousands of people. People who have never been to college or graduate school nor even finished high school are authoring books that impact the lives of millions. God is the one who exalts and promotes, and the effective leader understands that spiritual leadership is not self-assumed, but is God appointed.

Principle Five: *Effective Leaders are more interested in serving than in being served!*

Now the priest of Midian had seven daughters: and they came to draw water and filled the troughs to water their father's flock. Then the shepherds came and drove them away, But Moses stood up and helped them and watered their flock" (Exodus 2:16, 27).

Moses ran from the wrath of the Egyptian king and settled at the well where the seven daughters of the priest of Midian came to water their flock. Strong, handsome, powerful Moses who was accustomed to being waited on did something out of the ordinary, giving no thought to himself for personal gain he ran off the shepherds who accosted these daughters, and then, he watered their flocks.

One would look on the surface of this brief account and remark, "how the mighty have fallen." But on closer inspection, one sees that this event marks a dramatic shift in the emotional development of Moses. By taking the action he did, Moses swallowed the biggest piece of humble pie one could imagine. Remember that sheep and shepherds were considered low lives to the Egyptians. According to his training and the manner in which Moses had been raised coming to the aid of these seven women should have been the last thing he wanted to do, not to mention that the last time he had tried to help someone he was met with rejection. And look at the irony here, deliverance on a small scale. It is almost as if God was saying to Moses that if he had grandiose plans of being a deliverer that he had to begin here. He thought that he would be the deliverer of an entire nation, but he would begin being the deliverer of seven sisters and their sheep.

It is unfortunate how few leaders have any interest in being servants, but rather want to be served. Some pastors are prime transgressors. Their desire to be served is so great that they will have numbers of "armor bearers," "handmaidens", and "bodyguards" with earplugs for communication but pastor only a handful of people. Somehow many have forgotten the words of Jesus about himself, "For even the Son of Man did not come to be served, but to serve, and to give his life as a ransom for many" (Mark 10:25).

Moses, unlike many leaders in the contemporary faith community, was willing to be obscure. Once in the limelight of Egyptian society, he was now willing to dwell with the priest of Midian in anonymity. He no longer had to be the center of attraction. Things no longer had to be about him. He had become a servant!

Principle Six*: Effective Leaders know how to rest and rely on God.*

"Now it came about in the course of those many days that the king of Egypt died. And the sons of Israel sighed because of the bondage, and they cried out: and their cry for help because of their bondage rose up to God. So God heard their groaning; and God remembered His covenant with Abraham, Isaac, and Jacob. God saw the sons of Israel, and God took notice of them" (Exodus 2:23-25). We have no idea of how long Moses had been away from Egypt at the time this news reached his ears. We know that it was forty years in all before Moses would return to Egypt. We can surmise that his heart was touched and grieved when he heard of the condition of his people. However, rather than taking matters into his own hands, as he had done earlier, Moses rested and relied upon the Lord.

It is not easy to leave things in the hands of the Lord. We know that something has to be done and often times believe that we are the ones to do something about it, but proper timing says that God knows best what needs to be done, when it needs to be, and who it is that needs to do it. Often times our plans are a useless, senseless intrusion into the affairs of

God. What effective leaders need to do is rest and rely upon God. Don't be so quick to make plans, to strategies. The situation may call for a concerted season of prayer and fasting. It may call for silent reflection. I don't know how God will choose to move in a certain situation, but I do know that when something reaches the ears of God, God knows how to handle it. I may be laboring in confusion right now, not knowing where to turn, but one thing I do know is that God has the answer and if I turn to Him, learn to rest in Him, trust in Him, He will work it out.

Chapter Four

In the Fullness of Time

Everyone is always in such a hurry, impatient for things to happen according to some fixed schedule. We have become slaves to our calendars, day runners, daytimers and personal data assistants (P.D.A.s). We have timetables in our minds that drive our goals and aspirations. We anticipate accomplishing certain feats and arriving at certain places in our lives according to some unseen alarm clock, and are disappointed if we miss those markers.

I can remember planning my life anticipating that I would be married by a certain date, pastoring at a certain age, and have my doctorate by the time I was thirty. I was driven to accomplish these feats in the time I had determined I had to have them accomplished. No one was holding me to those markers but me, and hold to them I did. Of course, I did not meet any of those deadlines though I eventually accomplished each of those goals. As I think back on how I felt not accomplishing them in the time, I had arbitrarily determined I can remember feeling great pressure and anxiety. I can remember feeling a little like I had failed.

I have since discovered that there are many things God has for us in life that do not come according to our predetermined timetables, but rather they come in the fullness of time. Time is something with which we all struggle. Our western culture has made us slaves to time. Punctuality is seen as a virtue, and if you want to really frustrate someone, waste their time. I was confronted with how bound to and by time I really can be when I visited the Democratic Republic of the Congo for the first time. I was to be the evening featured preacher for a conference in the city of Kinshasa. Our hosts told me that they would be at the hotel to pick me up at 6:00 p.m., and so, in good Western fashion, I was dressed, ready and down waiting in the lobby at 5:45 pm. Yet, our hosts did not arrive for another hour. By the time we reached the church I was a nervous wreck, and yet our hosts were totally oblivious to my anxiety.

God is the God of time. God is the God in time. God is the creator of time, and God uses time for God's own special purposes. "One day is as a thousand years and a thousand years as a day." (2 Peter 3:8). God is not bound by the same time constraints that we are. God knows the beginning from the end. God knows what will happen before it happens, and God knows how it will end. He is not intimidated by time, for God was before there was time and He will be long after time as we know ceases to exist. Therefore, God has the capacity to take our finitude and make it infinite. We only see our limitations but God always sees our possibilities.

Moses, zealous to do something positive for his people, took matters into his own hands; and, in the process, totally miscalculated God's timing. That miscalculation cost him dearly. He lost his position in the royal court and suffering rejection from his own people, he lost his identity as an Israelite. Note that when he rescued the daughters of Jethro at the well they identified him as an Egyptian, not an Israelite. Moses had so missed the timing of God that he wound up doing the very thing that he had been taught was despicable for men, tending sheep.

Having imposed his own sense of timing upon the Israelites cost him everything, now Moses is living in the desert. But in the economy of God it, the desert, is the desert that turns out to be the best place for him to be. In the Hebrew the word for "desert" is *midbaar*. It is derived from the word *dahbaar*, meaning "to speak." This root term suggests that it is the desert that is the place where God is able to speak the most effectively to us. For all of its barrenness, all of its solitude, all of its loneliness, the desert is where, if one is able to listen, they will hear God speaking.

As we noted earlier, walking the flesh will land you in the desert. All of us at one time or another will spend time in the desert. For many time spent in the desert will be brief, just a short season. One may find them self in a financial desert but it is a short season of lack that will soon pass. Another may find them self walking through the valley of the shadow of death, and while the memory of one's loved one will never completely fade, life goes on, grief dissipates into fond memories, and sadness is replaced with joy. But Moses spends the next forty years in the desert. Forty years! Wrap yourself around that little fact for a moment. Moses, diplomat, statesman, military genius, so gifted, so talented is confined to the desert for forty years, raising two boys, ministering to his wife Zipporah and herding sheep. Why for some time in the desert is relatively brief but, for Moses, it was a whole generation and then some (a generation is generally considered to be thirty-five years)?

The key to time spent in the wilderness is directly linked to lessons needed to be learned. Moses was well trained in things that made him an expert in many fields. Yet, if he was to become the leader of a nation, he had to learn other lessons, and they were not taught in the University of Egypt. What was it that Moses had yet to learn?

Chuck Swindoll suggests that *Moses needed to learn the value of obscurity*. He had to learn what it meant to be a nobody. He had to learn how God deals with time. In his earlier attempt to be the people's deliverer, he had operated in his own sense of timing and was greatly mistaken.

Moses also had to learn about solitude, about silence. In the hustle, bustle life at the royal court, Moses had probably never been alone. There were undoubtedly servants forever present waiting on his every need, and there was likely no such thing as a quiet space. There are times in my life when I need noise, like noise, have to have noise to think. But there are other times when I have to have absolute silence. I cannot hear God when there are distractions on every side. Moses had to learn about solitude.

Finally, Moses had to learn about discomfort. All of his life he had dwelt in the lap of luxury. I assure you that there was nothing comfortable about Midian. Instead of the comfort of the royal palace, Moses dwelt in a tent as a Bedouin. Instead of a comfortable bed, he more than likely slept on the ground using skins and furs instead of silks and linens for covering.

Instead of the opulent baths, Moses had to contend with water from wells and oasises. It certainly was not the luxury he had become accustomed to having in Egypt.

God never does anything without a purpose. Moses learned much in the wilderness. He matriculated over the course of forty years, but "in the fullness of time," it was time for Moses to assume his position as deliverer of the Israelite people. The king was dead, and his successor was more cruel and demanding than he had been, and the people cried out to the Lord for help. God responds when you cry out to him for help. Their treatment over the years was harsh, but this is the first time that the Bible records that they cried out to the Lord. God waits for His people to call unto Him, and when they do He answers. God's answer for the Israelites, in the fullness of time, was the one that they had rejected forty years earlier. But was Moses ready? We will deal with that question in the next chapter. There are some principles we can glean from Moses time spent in the University of the Desert.

Principle One: *God seems to prefer using people who have failed.*

God uses whomever He predetermines to use to accomplish His purposes. God uses people who are unusually gifted, inordinately talented, and well prepared. Those that meet this short list of criteria are expected to to be used in leadership. That is why Saul was a natural as the first king of Israel. he looked like a king, walked like a king, talked like a king. He was tall and handsome. In fact, the Bible tells us that he stood a whole head taller than other men. Every physical piece of criteria that the world looks to in determining fitness for leadership Saul had it. He was a natural.

This same mentality toward fitness for leadership still exists. The American voter is fickled in selecting leaders. It tends to be drawn toward those who look like leaders and act like leaders. The person who is actually more fit to lead may never get elected because they did not adhere to the criteria that we look toward in selecting leaders. The selection process becomes more complicated when the elect of investigative journalism is added. Now not only does a candidate have to look, walk, talk, and act like a leader, they must be squeaky clean, have no skeletons in their closet. Who can forget the numbers of potential presidents who never made it because some indiscretion from their past was discovered and publicized.

I am grateful that God has a different standard when it comes to qualification for leadership. God looks beyond our faults and sees our need. He takes our sin and removes it from us as far as the east is from the west. He buries it beneath the deepest darkest sea, He remembers it no more. God does not condone our sin, but as James tells us, "if we confess our sin, God is faithful and just to forgive us and cleanse us from all wrong." So once we have sought and received forgiveness, it is as if nothing happened. God will never bring it up again. That is far different from the media's approach to what they consider to be news and the feeding frenzy of a population that craves the sensational. When I consider the sins of my past, while God has forgiven me, they would probably disqualify me from serving publicly.

God seems to prefer using people who have failed. When God called out to Moses from a bush that burned and yet was not consumed, He identifies Himself saying, 'I am the God of your father, the God of Abraham, the God of Isaac, and the God of Jacob.' The Moses hid his face, for he was afraid to look at God" (Exodus 3:6). What an intimidating list of powerful men who did mighty exploits for God. How could Moses ever identify with such a list, for that matter how can we? And yet when God mentioned their names, He was really saying that "I am the God of people like you who have failed and yet were still mightily used of me." These men were not the perfect stained glass window variety of saint that their names suggest. They were real people with real issues like the rest of us, and, like Moses.

I do not mean to imply that God does not use people who have not experienced failure in their lives, but He prefers to use people who have failed. I was reminded recently of my early days in pastoral ministry. I was twenty-five years old and on top of the world. I was a newly wed, new graduate and a new pastor. I had been groomed all my life to be a pastor, and while I had experienced some distress in my life I grew up mostly sheltered from the experiences most people testify to having been delivered from. As far as I was concerned I knew it all, no one could tell me anything. That misguided mentality almost destroyed my new marriage and nearly drove me from the pastorate. My problem was that with all of the minor drama I had experienced in my life, I did not really know what it meant to fail at something. I did not know what it meant to experience adversity, not real adversity. God used that first pastoral call to humble me through all the negative experiences and all the adversity and all the failure that I endured. God could not use me in the state I had been in. I was too self-absorbed, too self-assured, too self-confident, too self-sufficient.

The problem with failure, however, is that it makes one feels as though they are useless or worthless. Nobody likes failure. Failure forces us to reassess our goals and aspirations. It causes us to question whether we heard correctly from the Lord and allows the enemy of our souls the opportunity to tempt us into quitting and giving up because "if what we had attempted to do was, truly, of God, it would have succeeded." Sometimes we can see the deception of the enemy, but there are other times, times when we have been devastated by unexpected failure, that it is another matter entirely.

Failure is a part of life. There is no one that is without sin, "For all have sinned and come short of the glory of God" (Romans 3:23). Everyone one of us has a God-given destiny, a plan designed by the Lord of life for our lives, and if you are committed to walking in it, you had better get prepared for some failure. Everything will not always work out the way you want it to. There are going to be some miss-starts, some miscues and it will often come when you least expect it. You may get the "perfect job" and it not work out. You may meet the "perfect person" and the relationship goes nowhere. You may have your heart set on getting the new house or that new car, and nobody approves your loan request. You may finally get a good friend, and they let you down. Failure is a part of life, but failure is not final.

What do you think went through Moses' mind when he heard those words of God, "I am the God of your father. . ."? After forty years I am certain that all Moses could think about was his previous failure, and how that surely disqualified him from any role as deliverer of his people. Failure, unaddressed, as a way of paralyzing you into self-doubt and fear. The experienced of failure was at some earlier point in life may prevent an individual from attempting the thing they failed at again. Having experienced a nasty divorce after an ugly marriage may sour a person from getting married again. Having begun a business only to have to file bankruptcy may hinder a person from attempting another business. Having connected with a church and a pastor only to experience rejection and the reality of people's flesh in the people you looked up to and admired may deter one from every darkening the door of another church. That is the way the enemy paralyzes us, so we do nothing. But God was not content with letting Moses off that easy. He had a mission for him, and his earlier clumsy failure was qualification enough for God.

Principle Two*: God speaks to ordinary people in unpredictable ways.*

One of the saddest things for me to hear from another believer is dismay that God may actually speak to them. Their expectation is that God would, of course, speak to me, after all, it is my job. Those involved in professional ministry do not have a monopoly on hearing from God. In all honesty, God speaks to whomever God wants, simply because God is sovereign. God does not care who you are, what you have done, where or with whom you have been. We believe in the priesthood of all believers. That means that God can and does use those who have committed their lives to Him.

When God speaks, one cannot count on God speaking in predictable ways. It is important to pray daily, and it is important to read God's Word daily, but God may choose to remain silent during your times of prayer and study. God may decide to speak to you while you are riding in your car or out walking, or may awaken you in the middle of the night. It might happen that you hear God speaking directly to you through the voice of your spouse or your children, a good friend, a television program or a good book.

God appeared to Moses from a bush that was burning. Certainly, over the years, Moses had been accustomed to seeing bushes catch on fire in the wilderness, but they would generally burn out relatively quickly. So watching this fire, it is reasonable to conjecture that Moses expected the bush to burn out quickly. When it did not, and there was no indication that it would anytime soon, Moses had to investigate. God is unpredictable while at the same time being reliable, trustworthy and faithful. But God can and will use whatever is available to get our attention.

Principle Three*: God speaks using extraordinary events or circumstances to get our attention.*

"God is looking for someone with ears to hear His voice, hands ready to do HIs work, and a heart that is willing to respond" (Swindoll, pg. 109). The people of God and the church of which they are a part can make serving the Lord so complicated at times. Throughout the generations, there have been disputes in the church that have led to spin off movements and denominations, many of them over discerning the voice of God. There have been individuals and movements that have taken the attitude that God only speaks to certain persons or offices, thereby diminishing the ability of others to hear from God. The truth of the matter is that "The spirits of prophets are subject to the control of prophets" (1 Corinthians 14:32).

The issue is not so much about who can hear from the Lord as it is whether there is anyone who will hear from the Lord. Amidst the hustle and bustle of our chaotic world, most people have little time to hear from the Lord. We are generally so preoccupied with significant issues and events that we have neither the time nor the inclination to stop our routines long enough to hear from God. But God will be heard when He has a message to send to a person or to an individual, and if we are too "busy" to seek Him, then God will seek us sometimes using an extraordinary event or circumstance to tap us on the shoulder and get our attention.

For Moses, it was a bush that was on fire but appeared to not be consumed. Seeing this "marvelous sight, why the bush is not burned up," caused Moses to stop what he was doing and "turn aside" to investigate. The bush was not God, but it was that which God determined to use to get the attention of Moses. The text tells us that it was an angel of the Lord that appeared to Moses out of the bush, and get his attention it did. God knows how to get our attention when He has something to impart to us. The word of God will not always grab us in the usual manner. We may not hear what God wants is to hear sitting in the pew in the church we attend. It may not be while watching a gospel program, listening to gospel radio or music, or while reviewing an inspirational film. We may hear God speaking through unusual conduits, some of which may be secular, but all of which may happen in the course of common, ordinary, everyday circumstances. When was the last time God spoke to you? How did He get your attention? Was it through an accident? A lost job? A broken relationship?

Principle Four: *Things don't just happen!*

There are those that would have you believe that things in this life happen by chance. So they are quick to tell you when good things, perhaps unexpected things, come your way that you were "lucky." The whole of our society seems bent on operating according to chance. Just the other day, our state of North Carolina, in the state legislature, refused to offer the consideration of a statewide lottery for a statewide referendum. I honor the courageous legislators that boldly defied a growing cry to have what other states, including our neighbor to the south, South Carolina, already has. People will spend hundreds, even thousands of dollars trying to win something that offers little opportunity to win. Even a video basketball game we have been playing in my house offers the opportunity to bet on games and win money to buy more courts and more game gear. Operating by chance has become so popular that even my nine-year-old son offered to bet me on a game we were playing.

God does not do or allow things without a purpose. One theologian said that "God does not roll dice." One may not understand the purposes of God as it relates to a particular situation or circumstance, but God intends for something to come out of it nonetheless. The Deuteronomic writer says that we are either blessed with a blessing or cursed with a curse (Deuteronomy 28). That means that there is no middle ground with God, no point of compromise, no meeting us halfway.

The Apostle Paul writes, "And we know that in all things God works for the good of them that love Him and are called according to His purpose" (Romans 8:28). This is the assurance that we have that what we suffer from time to time has a purpose and though we do not understand it now, we know that somehow God is using it in His divine plan. Now I will be the first to admit that when you are going through a particularly trying time, it is hard to imagine how God can possibly use it for God's greater glory. In fact, it is hard to see how anything good can come out of it at all, yet the Word of God declares that things don't just happen.

I can imagine that when Moses experienced failure and rejection, then had to flee from his home for his life, that he wondered why he was suffering. I am certain that he had to wonder why things had not worked out the way he had hoped. I am sure that he was confused, and may have wondered where the god of his father, of Abraham, Isaac, and Jacob was then. Faced with the dramatic change from a pampered prince of Egypt to a lowly shepherd watching over flocks on the back side of the wilderness, Moses must have, surely, been perplexed about his fall from grace. I imagine that the last thing he considered was that all that he was going through was somehow in the providence of God. Yet, we now know that it was.

God used every bit of Moses' life for His glory, from his birth and education and upbringing in the royal household to his training in the university of the desert and his return to Egypt and subsequent sojourn in the wilderness. It was not readily apparent to Moses as it was happening, but in retrospect, we can God at work in every detail of his life. The same is true today for those who "love the Lord and are called according to His purpose." God is at work in every detail of our lives. I know that reading such words is difficult for some because you would wish on your worst enemy some of the things you have had to endure. Rest assured that God understands your hesitation, and is not intimidated by it. He does not cause your pain but surely uses it to accomplish His purposes, even if that means turning up the heat in your situation to get your attention. God wants to see His glory in us, so even the negative occurrences of our lives are fodder for God's glory.

Every trial and tribulation, every joy and blessing God is being used to accomplish His good and perfect will. Regardless of what many say who lack faith, or confessing believers who lack spiritual maturity, luck has nothing to do with the events of my life. Things don't just happen, but rather they happen according to the plan and design of a living God.

Chapter Five

Called By God

How does one get into Christian ministry? Is it a vocation or an advocation? Does one decide to choose Christian ministry in much the same manner as they would another profession or is there something special about how one winds up in ministry? These are important questions to ask in this day when there is such a shortage of spiritual leaders. There was a time when, in the mainline church, there were two vacancies for every candidate. Now there are two candidates for every vacancy, and the statistics are not encouraging when it comes to racial-ethnic candidates, particularly African American candidates. The shrinking pool of available candidates has caused denominational governing bodies to become more intentional in attracting potential candidates.

I am of the opinion, however, that much of our efforts in this area are out of line with the manner in which God calls women and men into ministry. Many of the approaches used to snare potential candidates are not much different from the recruiting strategies employed by the business and industry segments of our society. The prevailing attitude seems to be that the ordained ministry is no different than any other people profession, and so those who look and sound like clergy material are encouraged to pursue a career in ministry. The problem with this mentality is that when one goes at it like any other job, it does not take much to burn them out and ultimately run them out of the ministry altogether.

It is not uncommon for me to have the opportunity to address potential ministers, pastors, teachers, etc. I generally tell them that for one to go into the ministry full time, one either has to have taken leave of their senses or they have truly been called. The ministry, in fact, ministry in general, is often a lonely place. One may never get rich, and may never be appreciated to the degree they deserve, but when one has been called, none of that makes any difference.

I often heard my maternal grandmother comment about ministry, that it was filled with people in one of three categories, those that were called, those who were sent and others that just went. It is subjective to make the comparison that I am making, but my seminary experience proved that my grandmother right. There were many students in my seminary had no clue why there were there. Many finished college not knowing what they were going to do with their lives. With no desire to enter medical school or law school, seminary became the default. They were so clueless, in fact; I could not picture them leading anyone, let alone a congregation. Only concerted prayer and discerning preparation for ministry committees could spare the church from their future leadership.

Things have not changed much, though the majority of entering seminary students are second career people. There are many who enter full-time ministry for the wrong reasons. Some will enter the ministry because of some life-changing event. Others will do so because everybody and their brother were constantly pushing them toward it. The only sure fire way to know whether the ministry is for you is to know whether you have been called.

What does it mean to be called? What exactly are we talking about? Is "calling" one of those "church words" that nobody, including most Christians, understands? Is it like that of Moses, who heard the voice of God through a bush that burned and yet was not consumed? Is it like that of Amos who was taken from following the flock to leading *the flock*? Perhaps it was like that of Isaiah who saw the Lord high and lifted up with God's train filling the temple, and heard angels crying "holy," and whose lips were anointed by a burning coal?

When I remember my calling it was like none I mentioned above. Instead, it was more of an inward impression, a strong sense of purpose. I cannot explain it, but I knew without a doubt that I had been called to minister. There were times when I added the prospect of being or doing something else, but I never lost my thirst for ministry. Now my experience is not like that of others, and the experience of Moses is dramatically different from others. Most people struggle long and hard with their calling to ministry.

Moses heard God speaking in a clear and audible way. In

that way, he is very different. But though he heard God speaking directly to him, he struggled nonetheless. If it had been me, the bush burning would have been enough to convince me, but it was not enough for Moses. Moses resisted offering up excuse after excuse for why God must surely have been mistaken. In this way Moses is like the most of us. We may never be called to full-time ordained Christian ministry, but we have been called to full-time ministry, and we constantly struggle with that calling. Look at the way that Moses struggled. Some commentators list five excuses, others list just four. I like the way Chuck Swindoll lists them: "I don't have all the answers," "I may not have their respect," "I'm slow in my expressions," and "I'm not as qualified as others." Four excuses all designed to say the same thing to God, "You must have the wrong one." Let us look at them more closely, as principles.

Principle One: *Effective Spiritual Leaders know that they do not have all the answers.*

One of the most infuriating things I have experienced is encountering a person that knows everything. I do not know whether you have ever run into such a person, but the experience can be so traumatic that you regret to see that person come your way. It does not matter what you are talking about they have had some experience with it that makes them expert in that particular area. It is one thing to have an opinion about a given subject matter, but no one knows everything about everything, which means that everyone should not have an opinion about everything, that is not an informed opinion.

I have often wondered why someone would behave as though they have all the answers. I have no desire to be seen as someone's personal encyclopedia. But I suppose that some person's desire to be esteemed and appreciated could conceivably motivate them to behave in such an illogical manner. I say illogical because once a person sets them self up as having all the answers, they foster unreasonable personal expectations and exposes them self to disappointment and grave embarrassment when it is discovered that they do not know it all.

The movie entitled, "Water Boy," starring Adam Sandler comically, yet, vividly illustrates this point. Adam's character having been raised in a sheltered, backwards environment grows into adulthood believing that his mother had all the answers. It became quickly apparent that every time his mother did not have the correct answer, or desired to shelter him from the truth, she made something up. Adam's character was made to look like more of an imbecile than he actually was when he discovered the folly of his mother's deception.

One cannot be too critical of this character's mother, for the temptation is great to act more knowledgeable than one actually is when in a position of leadership. I can remember when my children were very young and in that stage in which they questioned everything. They asked questions because they thought that, certainly, I had the answers. Then, when they started school, they would seemingly test me asking only the questions for which they already had the answers. When a child is constantly asking questions it is easy to give inaccurate answers to appease them, especially after admitting you did not know and they want to know why you did not know.

It is not necessary for leaders to know all the answers. One of the most helpful things I learned in my graduate school education was not knowing all the answers, but knowing where to look to find them. I have discovered that people appreciate receiving honest answers to their straight forward questions. They may not simply settle for "I don't know," but will accept the "I don't know" if it is accompanied by a commitment to find an answer.

The first excuse that Moses gave God was, "Suppose I go to the Israelites and say to them, 'The God of your fathers has sent me to you,' and they ask me, 'What is his name?' Then what shall I tell them?" What Moses was really saying was, "I can't go as your spokesperson. The people will ask me some hard questions and I won't have the answers and I will look stupid." Moses was revealing what is a basic flaw in human nature, the supposition that we are sufficient in and of ourselves for all things. Though much has changed in thousands of years; we suffer from the same flaw. Many called into leadership are still making lame excuses and nothing but "pride" gets in our way. Proverbs tells us that "a haughty spirit goes before a fall and pride before destruction."

Moses missed what many leaders still miss; it is not necessary to have all the answers. Effective spiritual leaders know that they do not have all the answers. Note God's response, "I AM WHO I AM. This is what you are to say to the

Israelites: 'I AM has sent me to you.'" God was saying to Moses you don't need to have all the answers, you won't have all the answers, but you will have all of me.

That is great news. The pressure is off to be self-sufficient. I don't have to have all the answers, because I have all of the Lord. The Lord of the universe is with me, has called me, appointed me, sent me. I represent the one preexistent, self-existent, sovereign, infinite being in the universe.

Principle Two: *Effective Spiritual Leaders Manage Their Fear of Rejection*

Watching leaders standing in front of people seems easy enough until one gets the opportunity to stand in their shoes for a short time. It is then that one discovers how difficult it is to lead. Nothing is more humbling, and at times more humiliating, than attempting to lead people, especially the people of God. While we know that God has not given us a spirit of fear, fear is real. It is natural to wonder how you are being perceived, how you are being received. No one looks forward to being rejected, yet I would be less than honest if I did not tell you that rejection is something I constantly have to manage. Every time I stand before God's people I am confronted with this fear. Every time I enter a new venue, encounter new people or introduce a new idea with those who are familiar, I am assaulted with this fear.

A leader who gives in to their fear will be paralyzed and attain little or nothing for the Kingdom of God. That it is one of the strategies employed by the enemy of our souls in this hour. People need leaders, even desire them, but paralyze the community and the leader are hindered from progressing in the things of God. Now fear in and of itself is not bad. It is one of the things that keeps the people of God honest. The day I no longer have to manage my fear is the day that I reassess whether I am operating in the will of God, and walking by faith. The fear reminds me that I am incapable of accomplishing anything for the Lord in and of my own wisdom, knowledge, intellect, and strength, but I cannot allow it to conquer me.

Fear is real, but it not what God gives, and if God is not the one who gives it then we know its origin. Paul tells his son in the ministry, Timothy, that "God has not given us the spirit of fear, but the spirit of love, power, and a sound mind." I laid my hands on you, but you received nothing from me, it was imparted by God. It came as a breath, a blast from God himself and as it is in me, it is in you. Paul says that God did not give us a "spirit" of fear, but a "spirit" of . . . The Greek word used for spirit is *"pneuma"* which means breath or blast, a current of air. Something that was put in us. But it also carries the connotation of "mental disposition."

We did not receive a spirit of fear (*"deilia"* is used only one time in the New Testament) which means timidity, fear or fearfulness, and denotes cowardice was not given to us. We did receive a spirit of power (*dunamis* – used 112 times in NT) which means ability, abundance, might and specifically refers to miraculous power given to us. Look at Mark 16:17-8: "And these signs will accompany those who believe: In my name they will drive out demons; they will speak in new tongues; they will pick up snakes with their hands; and when they drink deadly poison, it will not hurt them at all; they will place their hands on sick people, and they will get well."

We did receive a spirit of love (*agape'* – used 106 times in NT) which means the love of God shown toward us in the giving of His Son. But as it relates to our love for one another it is not an impulse from the feelings, it does not always run with the natural inclinations, it seeks the welfare of all, it works no ill toward any, it seeks the opportunity to do good to all, especially to those who belong to the household of faith. We did receive a spirit of self-discipline or self-control (*sophronismos* – from sophron which means literally "saving the mind", it is used one time in the NT) is actually an admonishment or calling to soundness of mind or to self-control.

It is this spirit of love, power, and soundness of mind that gives us what we need to manage the fear of rejection. Moses could have benefited from knowing what we now know. He did not know how to manage his fear, and so he gave into it. His second excuse was mostly hypothetical, it began with the words "what if. . ." Chuck Swindoll says that those are forever the words of worriers. Moses was worried about all the things that could possibly happen. In fact, he was so concerned about the hypothetical possibilities that could not hear what God was saying. What Moses did not understand is that God understood his fear, He understood his pain. When God has called you to a particular task, you do not need to labor in fear over the various possible scenarios. God is God and He is in charge. But to respond to Moses' concerns God enabled him to perform three awesome miracles.

The first miracle was taking his staff turning it into a serpent and them back again into a staff. The second miracle turned Moses' hand leprous and then whole again. In the third miracle, Moses would take water from the Nile and turn it into blood. By these three miracles, the Israelites would have to know that Moses was for real. One miracle alone could be construed as a cheap parlor trick, but all three was a tremendous validation of Moses' ministry and mission. God knows how to validate you. If God has truly called you there is no need to attempt to authenticate or validate yourself. Nor is there reason to fear how you will be received. God has already paved the way for your acceptance, and should you be rejected the ones to whom you have been sent are not rejecting you, but the One who sent you.

Principle Three*: Effective Spiritual Leaders Trust God in the Communication of Words.*

It can be terribly intimidating to stand and speak before crowds of people, especially ones that you may not know or ones that know something negative about you. Moses certainly had to have had in mind the fact that he was a murderer and a fugitive from justice, and that the people would surely remember. I suppose that he surmised that there was no way he could be accepted as a leader, let alone as a speaker. So he protested to the Lord, "I have never been eloquent, neither in the past nor since you have spoken to your servant. I am slow of speech and tongue" (4:10)

It is an interesting protest especially when you consider the words of Stephen in the book of Acts. Stephen maintains that rather than being "slow of speech and tongue," Moses was instead "powerful in speech and action" (Acts 7:22). Here is an apparent contradiction. Which is true? Was Moses possessed of some type of speech impediment, or was he an eloquent orator? One writer maintains that Moses was once an effective, powerful communicator, but that when he experienced the rejection that he did he "lost his touch" (Getz, pg. 57). Moses was actually in a form of denial. Before he had to flee as a fugitive from Egypt, Moses knew that he was destined for more than he could see. But after he had left the environment of Egypt where he was intellectually stimulated on a daily basis he was limited to the isolation and solitude of a shepherd in the wilderness. He no longer had the educational opportunities, regular dialogues with some of the brightest scholars in the then known world. He was severed from constant exposure to cutting edge information and knowledge. It is entirely probable that Moses simply slipped into a type of malaise that prevented him from communicating well. Some scholars believe that he might have developed a stutter.

I can well understand how an environment can cause a person to regress if there is no intentional effort to "keep up." Someone once commented on the change they would see in me when I would leave the environment of urban ministry and step back into the academic environment. I am the same person, but my language changes, my vocabulary changes, my style of communicating the gospel changes, all because of the environment. I have often noted with chagrin that my speech professor would be greatly disappointed to hear how my language has regressed over the years I have pastored in the inner city. Moses spent forty years, a full half of his life away from the environment that had nurtured him, to now go back into that environment was more than a little intimidating, and so he protests, "I have neither been eloquent. . . I am slow of speech and tongue."

What we should learn from Moses is that when God calls one to a particular task whatever deficiencies they might have or believe that they have are of little consequence. God knows how to take little and make much. God knew what Moses was capable of doing and being, and God knows what you and I have in us. Every time I rise to speak, in fact, as I write these words, I am confronted with my own sense of inadequacy, yet I know that God is able to use my words for His glory. So I trust Him to not only order my steps but my thoughts and words also. I trust Him to place the right words in my mouth even when they seem ineffective. I trust Him because I know that God knows how to accomplish His will and bring glory to Himself.

Now there are no shortcuts for proper preparation. The day I become accustomed to "winging it" is the day I discover how inadequate I really am. God wants us to do the hard work of preparation. An anonymous writer wrote these words and I have heard Bishop T. D. Jakes intone them more than once in the company of preachers who are used to communicating the Word: "Study yourself full, think yourself clear, pray yourself hot, and let yourself go." The person that bypasses this process in attempting to communicate the Word of God to the people of God is courting disaster. They may discover that God who sees you moving out in front of Him alone may leave you alone and on your own.

> ***Principle Four:*** *Effective Spiritual Leaders Know that it is Futile to Resist the Call of God.*

The fourth and final excuse that Moses uses is the most pathetic of all: "O Lord, please send somebody else to do it" (4:13). Up until this point God had been patient with Moses. He answered everyone of His objections and reassured him every step of the way. But now after everything God has done to reassure Moses and motivate him to accept the mantle of leadership, Moses essentially pleads for the Lord to send someone else to do it. Moses was so thoroughly intimidated by the call that anybody but him would have been a better candidate, or so at least he thought.

On the surface, it appears rather difficult to argue with God in the manner that Moses does here. Perhaps most who read this words would protest that they would never dare to question God in this way, and yet that is precisely what we do with such fluid persistence that we hardly notice that we are guilty of doing it all. Every time we elevate our agenda before the Lord's, regardless of the importance we may attach to it, we are guilty of resisting the call of God. Every time we gloss by what we hear in our spirit because we think that there is someone else better suited we are resisting the call of God.

I think that everyone has been guilty of resisting God at some point in their life and can attest to the fact that God knows how to get our attention and draw us back to what He has called us to do. I can remember going off to a "little five" type college is the Midwest and finding myself in the midst of well to do students. Many came to college driving high dollar cars and all I had was a ten-speed bicycle. I knew that I was called to the pastorate but quickly became envious of their money and their seeming lack of concern for how to pay their tuition or for anything they wanted. It was not long before I put my faith on the back burner intent on going now to law school and making some money. The Word of God is sure when it says that "the love of money is a root of all evil." That love took me from my first love. But God was persistent and would not let me go. During my junior year the Lord got a hold of me and turned me around and, today, I am serving where God wants me.

Effective spiritual leaders know the folly of trying to resist God. God got angry at Moses and gave him his brother as a spokesperson. God gave Moses what he wanted, what would placate him, but Moses ended up with more trouble from Aaron than he wanted. I am certain that Moses would say, "don't bother to try and resist. Just give in and trust God to do great things through you."

To be called by God from the darkness of our sin into the marvelous light of His grace is the lot of all who name the name of Jesus as their Lord and Savior. It is a calling each of us are well equipped in which to operate. No matter how complex or specific the call by virtue of our relationship with Jesus we already have what we need to be effective. Moses was not convinced that he was sufficiently prepared. He thought God had the wrong one in mind and so resisted when He called. But how can the high King of Heaven be mistaken? When God issues a call He is acutely aware of the strengths and the weaknesses of the one(s) He has called, and even if the gifts of that person are not equal to the task God knows how to supply what is needed.

I know from personal experience what it is to second guess myself and, by extension, God. But I have discovered that God knows what is best for me. he knows where He wants me to be and what He wants me to do. He knows my frailties, my fears, my anxieties, my shortcomings, and is never intimidated by them. If God can make a donkey speak, if He can take rocks and trees and cause them to cry out, then He can certainly take me and use me for His glory. So when I arrive at the end of the day, when I hang my robe back in the closet and pack my bags to go home, while I naturally will wonder how effective I have been I also know that it is not my ultimate concern, because God is in control of the results.

So boldly get up and walk into your calling. Don't resist, don't doubt, don't be afraid. The Lord your God is with you, and He will aid you in your ministry to be an effective spiritual leader. Now that does not mean that things will be easy. In fact, there are consequences to be paid as we walk faithfully in our callings. Moses discovered those consequences and yet still persisted. In the next few chapters, we will address those consequences and how we can persist in doing the work of the Lord in spite of them.

Chapter Six

Consequences

There was a time in my pastoral ministry when it was easy to get people to step forward and take leadership. The process of selection was extremely archaic and proved little more than a popularity contest. It was clear that many who agreed to serve as leaders had not fully considered what such a decision would entail. Over time, through teaching and training, it became increasingly difficult to get people to serve. While it proved, at times, troublesome, lacking the number of leaders needed to effectively shoulder the load, I stopped being overly concerned because people were finally beginning to take seriously their roles.

Whenever one decides to affirmatively answer the call to positions of leadership there are always consequences. Far too many people have underestimated the level of commitment leadership requires, much in the same way that many parents underestimated the commitments parenting would require. Whenever I would complain about things occurring with my children I would suddenly be reminded that I asked to be a parent and much of what I complained about simply came with the job. Now that is not particularly good news for anyone with a romanticized view of parenting or any other leadership role. Things have a tendency to look easier from a distance. Someone watches a leader operate effectively in their role (or ineffectively as the case may be) and assumes that what they have observed is easily done. One quickly discovers, however, that the task of leadership is more difficult than they had imagined, and that there unexpected consequences that accompany one's commitment to step forward into leadership. There are consequences relative to time, resources

It is not uncommon to have people in leadership positions who accepted the role because of a perception that was false. Some will agree to lead believing that doing so will not only give them added authority and power, but also the admiration, respect, and esteem of the people. The truth of the matter is that the leader who is diligent in performing their tasks may be despised and rejected by the ones they seek to serve. Taking the role of a leader can, often times, be a solitary existence, particularly if that role is in ministry. If one is accustomed to enjoying close relationships with coworkers they may discover that such relationships are difficult with those whom they are leading.

The manner in which an individual is viewed changes once that person takes on a leadership role. Yanked from obscurity, the new leader now becomes open game for the critical and the fault finders. Every decision or indecision becomes an item of debate. Everything from the clothing the leader wears, the house and neighborhood in which they live, and the manner in which they speak become items of public discussion. Many times I have heard people in leadership complain of feeling as though they have no life of their own.

I had not considered the possible consequences I would face when I first began to pastor. I am totally unprepared for what I would face in my first pastoral experience. The first Monday morning in the first congregation I served I ran headlong into said unexpected consequences. An elderly lady, daughter of a preacher, a retired university professor called me to her house. I thought I was going to visit, but when I arrived I was handed a 3x5 index card containing every word I had mispronounced the day before in my first Sunday morning service as the "new" pastor. This dear lady, whom we affectionately called (behind her back) "the bride of Frankenstein" (she wore a salt and pepper beehive hairdo with a white streak up the middle), proceeded to advise me on the proper way to do everything from baptisms to communion. She was not the least bit hesitant to give me the benefit of her wisdom because as the daughter of a preacher she felt unusually qualified to do so.

Years later this episode is comical, but at the time it was devastating to a young pastor. I did not know how to respond to her and could have allowed the experience to drive me from that to which I knew I had been called. I remembered however that those that would be leaders live in glass houses. In other words, there are consequences to accepting your calling. Now

I would never argue that what this lady did to me, and what others have done to countless numbers of leaders was right, or that the proper response is to just take it. I should have lovingly, but firmly set this lady in her place, and because I did not she continued to be a thorn in my side for the duration of that pastorate.

In the life of Moses once he had surrendered to the call of God on his life we see the beginning of the consequences he would encounter as a result of that decision. These consequences began rather benignly but progressively became more acute as time went by. The greater the stakes of the task to which a person has been called the greater the consequences associated with it. It should be noted that the enemy of our souls has a vested interest in keeping us distracted from walking in our anointing. How one perceives the consequences they face has a great impact on whether a person can weather them or whether they will throw in the towel and quit concluding that the price is too high.

For Moses, those consequences struck close to home right away. After forty years he had to pack up his family and leave. He had to face the prospect of losing a son because of an unfulfilled obligation, and he had to brief his brother, whom he had not seen for forty years, on a mission he had just received. He had to face the uncertain reception of a people and grow comfortable operating in a miraculous gifting with which he was unfamiliar. Then there was the initial encounter with the Pharaoh that produced disastrous results and caused the people whom he had come to deliver added pain and suffering which they then took out on him. There are some principles leaders can learn from Moses that will enable all that accept positions of leadership to serve more confidently and effectively.

Principle One: *Leaders must leave their past to embrace their future.*

After Moses' last excuse and his final plea that God get somebody else for the job, he finally surrendered to God's will and quit protesting. Then he went to his father-in-law and asking to be released from his responsibilities so he could return to Egypt. Moses did not ask for a leave of absence. He did not ask for his uncle to watch over his family while he went on a business trip. Moses understood that God was calling him to something that was going to entail tremendous commitment. So when Moses went to his uncle he knew that he was not likely to return. God had made a change in his life. He knew that it was time for him to leave behind those things over which he no longer had any control.

Many people in ministry leadership positions believe they can hold on to the past, even duplicate it, if only they had a greater level of commitment from the people they lead. As long as a person persists in living in the past they will be prevented from moving into the future. I recognize that there are numerous people who are resistant to change. They will hold on to their past, therefore, because it is easy and comfortable. Their past is familiar. They know what to expect. The future is an unknown. But it is the unknowns in which God specializes.

God cannot effectively use those who will not step out in faith. Those who would lead have to be willing to follow God's leading especially when it is challenging.

One way to easily see where a leader has not left their past is in their relationships. Everything about us changed when we came into a relationship with the Lord. We could not continue to relate to people in the same way that we always had because God had done something new in us. Many new Christians have been drawn back into the snare of the enemy because they could not turn their backs on their pasts. For leaders the change is even more critical, now there are others following for whom they are responsible. It is not that the relationships cease, but they do change.

For instance, the person that frequented after-hours clubs and bars cannot continue to do so and give spiritual leadership to a flock of believers. Drunken carousing into the wee hours of the morning is incompatible with leading people into their destiny and their promise. Once I committed my life to giving spiritual leadership, all the old givens of my life had to change. Now I know that I am slipping over into some issues of holiness, but leaders must lead by example. My Bible tells me that we are to "avoid the appearance of evil." It is critical that we leave the past behind and move toward the future because we never know who is watching our lives; who it is that might be gauging their decision on whether or not to trust in Jesus Christ as their personal Lord and Savior on how we live our lives.

I am not afraid of the word "holiness". God says, "You shall be holy because I am holy." Unfortunately, some equate holiness with a particular denomination or group instead of seeing it as the lifestyle to which God calls all Christians. I am not making a plea for perfection, for that is not what holiness is. Rather I am making a plea for separation. That brings me to the next principle.

Principle Two: *God has a higher standard for leaders than for others.*

In this fourth chapter, there is a couple of verses where the text reads that God was about to kill Moses. Some commentators maintain that it was not Moses God was about to kill, but one of his sons. Others contend that God was going to kill Moses himself because he had failed to circumcise one of his sons. I agree with the those who suggest that it was Moses' son God sought to kill especially since God had gone to such extremes to motivate Moses to accept his calling. It would seem to be a minor infraction for which Moses was being held accountable, but it illustrates how serious God is about what He requires.

According to Genesis 17:9-14, the covenant God had with Abraham involved circumcision, a cutting of the foreskin of the penis. Abraham, and every male in his family for all future generations were to undergo this procedure. It was a sign of the covenant between God had with His people. By engaging in the practice, Abraham, and the generations of males after him were signifying that the Lord alone would be their God and they would trust and serve Him. God had committed himself in a similar fashion (Genesis 15:7-21) through this covenant.

The ancient covenant was solemnized by slaughtering an animal, arranging halves of the carcasses opposite each other, and walking down the aisle between the halves. The practice signified a self-maledictory oath: "May it be so done to me if I do not keep my oath and pledge." The practice was obligatory and God was so emphatic about it being done that God said, "Any uncircumcised male, who has not been circumcised in the flesh will be cut off from his people; he has broken my covenant"(Genesis 17:14). Most ancient covenants were sealed in blood making it a blood covenant. The family and friends in a wedding party waited outside the wedding chamber for the marriage to be consummated to validate that the bride was, indeed, a virgin. If there was no blood on the bed coverings the covenant was nullified and the bride stoned to death. So the wedding night becomes a blood covenant.

With Moses having not circumcised one of his sons he had broken the covenant, and his son had to be cut off. Now on the surface, it does not seem to be fair that God would deal with Moses in this fashion. To some, it would seem that God was a little less than charitable in the way in which this was handled. It simply highlights to me how serious leadership is and how serious God takes it and wants us to take it. That God was set to kill the boy tells me that God wanted Moses to know God's standard and live by it. For Moses, that standard was so great and the call of God on his life so strong; he would miss physically crossing the Jordan River into the promised land because he struck a rock for water in anger. It doesn't seem fair does it?

It highlights for me, however, how ridiculous the debates in the church about ordination standards really are. Those who lobby for a reinterpretation of the Bible as it related to sexuality do so out of a sense of wanting to live their lives like everyone else. Yet God has called and is still calling, leaders to a higher standard. Ministry leaders cannot be like everyone else. There are places I will not frequent, things I will not do, things I will not say because God has a higher standard and higher expectation of me than of others.

Leaders cannot lead people where they do not go or have not been. They will not have it all together; they are as fallible as the next person. Yet what is required of all Christians is especially incumbent on them because of their office. There is so much carnality among Christian leaders that the world has difficulty distinguishing between them and those in the broader society. Unless leaders seriously grasp the principle of adhering to a higher standard they run the risk of being cut off from their people.

> ***Principle Three:*** *It is important to have ministry partners upon whom you can depend.*

When God decided to kill Moses' son, Zipporah, Moses' wife, intervened. Thank God for effective partners in ministry. recognizing that God was disturbed about this breach of His covenant, Zipporah quickly rectified the problem by circumcising the son and bringing the foreskin as evidence to

Moses. This gruesome and graphic account highlights clearly, I think, the importance of effective ministry partners.

Good ministry partners—whether spouses or coworkers—are important and often hard to find. Leaders often times miss important details that can effectively stifle what God is doing. A good ministry partner is that extra set of eyes and ears to pick up and give counsel in those things that have been missed.

Of all the partners in ministry one can have, it is generally the spouse that proves the most valuable. Often times we may have to get past our ego to receive counsel from them, but rarely are they too far off. Whether it is a person or a situation that intimate ministry partner is able to point out the possible pitfalls, the liabilities as well as the benefits.

I can also point to the folly of having partners in ministry that are anything but effective. One of the most frustrating parts of ministry is having to deal with those who make great promises but fail to follow through. That is not only frustrating, but it is often accompanied by a tremendous sense of betrayal. One of the great mistakes that I have made in my personal ministry is not adequately empowering leaders to lead and then not holding them accountable. My disposition was such that if a person did not follow through on what they had committed to doing then I would do it myself. Two things happened: people grew accustomed to me doing what they should have done and I got overly tired and began to feel bitter.

I remember hearing Bishop T.D. Jakes teach on the part of the text in which God gives Moses his staff and shows him what it was capable of doing [Exodus 4:2-4]. For Jakes, the casting of the staff on the ground and it becoming a snake symbolizes how leaders need to throw down their "staffs", assign them specific responsibilities, and expect them to wiggle. If they don't, then, clearly, that the leader has the wrong staff. Many leaders tolerate mediocrity in their ministries because of ineffective staff. One can never be as their most effective and influential without partners that can be counted on.

If we evaluate the partnership Moses had with his brother Aaron, we see something interesting. In the fourth chapter, the Lord told Aaron, 'Go into the desert to meet Moses.' So he met Moses at the mountain of God and kissed him. Then Moses told Aaron everything the Lord had sent him to say, and also about all the miraculous signs he had commanded him to perform' (vs. 27, 28). The meeting of Moses and Aaron occurred as a result of Moses' insistence that he was not the right person for the job, that he could not articulate well and that the Lord really needed to get someone else for the job. So God connects Moses with his own brother Aaron who becomes Moses' mouthpiece. God connected them as partners, though not equal partners, in ministry; but Aaron would prove to be less than effective. In fact, Aaron would prove to be easily manipulated and Moses would live to regret that God had put them together as partners in ministry. It's important to be connected with the right person(s) or your ministry will be aborted before it gets going.

Principle Four: *When awaiting change, things tend to get worse before getting better.*

Of the many myths to which we subscribe there are few more insidious than maintaining that God-ordained change should come easy. In my years of pastoring, I have had people to challenge the fact that a particular change was not going well as a sign that it was not in the providence of God There is nothing further from the truth. It is a tremendous blessing from God when change occurs smoothly. Yet, generally, change is accompanied by resistance and opposition because the enemy of our souls fights against the people and things of God.

Moses and Aaron arrived in Egypt, brought together the elders of the people, shared with them everything the Lord had told them, received their support, shared in their joy, appeared before the Pharaoh to present their petition, then promptly ran into a buzz saw. Rather than the king responding positively their request, which was simply to allow the Israelites time to hold a festival to the Lord in the desert, he made their task of producing bricks more difficult by cutting their supply of straw. Now they had to produce the same quota of bricks as before but had to collect their own supply of straw wherever they could find it. And, suddenly euphoria over the fact that the Lord had seen their misery and a deliverer turned into anger, disdain, and frustration.

The Israelite's dilemma then is the same as it is today for the people of God. They suffered from the delusion that change should happen smoothly and without opposition. Change never happens smoothly, especially when the change that is anticipated involves money. The king of Egypt saw what Moses was requesting as an assault on the economy of the nation, and his hatred for their race caused him to be punitive in his response. One should never be caught by surprise when opposition comes in response to proposed change. Rather, opposition and resistance should be expected. That opposition and resistance should be expected to be more pronounced before things get better.

I heard a pastor talking about change as part of a cycle of growth. The cycle was so simple and to the point that it was scary. It goes something like this: healthy things grow, growing things change, change challenges us, challenge forces us to trust God, trust leads to obedience, obedience makes us healthy, and healthy things grow. Change is a part of life. If something is healthy it will grow and it will change. The Egyptians enslaved the Israelites when they saw them growing into a mighty nation that could possibly challenge them militarily themselves or by allying themselves with their enemies. The change that occurred as a result of their growth brought a great challenge, and those challenges grew more pronounced and acute as time went by before they experienced their deliverance.

Leaders in the church of Jesus Christ need to hear and understand that that same cycle operates in the lives of individuals as well as it does in the organizations and groups they lead. If a group, an organization is healthy it can expect to grow. [Groups that are not experiencing growth need to determine where they are not healthy.] Growth is going to bring change, and because people do not react to change well, it will bring challenges as well. We should not be frightened of the challenge because "we walk by faith and not by sight." Challenges should simply point us to trust God more—Trust that God knows what is best for us. Trust that God is leading the way. Trust that we are on the right track.

If we can trust God, we will walk in obedience to His will. I find it easy to obey those whom I trust. I do not have to see to believe if I trust you, and then it is my obedience that makes me healthy, and the whole cycle begins again.

The principle that things tend to get worse before they get better is still true, but, by itself, it is misleading, because it is merely part of the cycle. If I can keep this cycle in my mind, I am not frustrated by the challenges because I know what is coming next. We allow the challenges of life to stop our progress toward destiny. We allow them to derail that which God has already done and is doing in our lives. The enemy of our souls wants us to become frustrated and quit, but remember he is a liar. Moses and Aaron did not quit. Instead, they went to the Lord and God was able to let them see that Pharaoh's response was simply part of His grand design. Now they were about to see God's mighty hand at work. Can you trust God enough in your situation to wait to see His mighty hand at work?

Chapter Seven

In the Hands of A Living God

With the exception of the resurrection, there is perhaps no greater demonstration of the awesome power of God than the plagues visited upon the nation of Egypt. When one reads the account they are struck by the severity of the plagues and must surely wonder what possible purpose could God have had for inflicting them upon this nation. There were ten plagues in total, each of them more devastating than the previous one, and each of which was intended by God to soften the stubborn heart of the Egyptian king. There was a further purpose for the plagues, and this may sound a bit extreme, to build the fragile self-esteem of Moses and prepare him for the forty years that was to come.

Moses was a broken man. We see evidence of his lack of self-esteem in his resistance to the call of God on his life. This once self-assured man was now suspicious of his talents and his gifts, a stark contrast to the confidence he exuded when he was a prince in Egypt and sought to right what he saw as a wrong and killed one of the Egyptian taskmasters. Forty years on the back side of wilderness with little more company than the flock of sheep he shepherded was sufficient to cause him to doubt what was once evident to all, his ability to lead. God used the plagues to build Moses to the stature of the man he had created, blessed, anointed and appointed. When Moses first encounters Pharaoh Aaron is operating as his spokesperson, Aaron is handling the staff and performing the miracles at Moses' instruction. But by the time we reach the fourth plague Aaron is no longer speaking for Moses, but now Moses is speaking for himself. Clearly, his self-esteem has been rebuilt.

Perhaps, as an intended effect of the plagues, it was also in the plan of God that these plagues would rebuild the faith and confidence of the Israelites who had become increasingly acculturated to the Egyptian lifestyle and pagan worship. Surely no one witnessing these plagues would dare to doubt the power of God to change the course of events in the lives of people and nations. The Israelites would need faith and confidence to be able to survive and endure what was ahead for them.

What happened in Egypt was no accident, afterthought, reflexive reaction, or last-minute exception to God's plan for the deliverance of Egypt. God knew beforehand that the king was stubborn and that the only way to get his attention was through this extreme method.

"But I know that the king of Egypt will not let

you go unless a mighty hand compels him. So I will stretch out my hand and strike the Egyptians with all the wonders the at I will perform among them. After that, he will let you go." (Exodus 3:19, 20)

"The Lord said to Moses, 'When you return to Egypt, see that you perform before Pharaoh all the wonders I have you the power to do. But I will harden his heart so that he will not let the people go.'" (Exodus 4:21)

"But I will harden Pharaoh's heart, and though I multiply my miraculous signs and wonders in Egypt, he will not listen to you. Then I will lay my hand on Egypt and with mighty acts of judgment I will bring out my divisions, my people the Israelites. And the Egyptians will know that I am the Lord when I stretch out my hand against Egypt and bring the Israelites out of it," (Exodus 7:3-5)

God knew that this was one king who had a stubborn heart. Nothing short of these devastating plagues was going to affect this man. Repeatedly we see the king seemingly unaffected by the often gruesome, always tragic impact of the plagues on his own people. So the plagues were as much a part of God's master plan of deliverance for the Israelite people as the calling of Moses or the Exodus itself.

The Egyptian people ultimately had to pay the price for

their king's stubbornness. The entire nation found itself in the hands of a living God. Repeatedly, throughout the text, we read the word "all", "all the land, all the livestock, all the men and beasts, all the firstborn." But the "all" referred only to the Egyptians. Every time God inflicted a plague on the people, the land of Goshen and the Israelite people were miraculously exempted from the plagues. It was as though they were living within a special fall out shelter. God's judgment was on the Egyptian people, and specifically on the Egyptian king.

Let us look more closely at the plagues themselves. As I stated above, there were ten plagues in all. One commentator concludes that they all took place in the course of one month. The plague of blood, the eighteenth day of the sixth month(Exodus 7:14-18); the plague of frogs, the twenty-fifth day of the sixth month (Exodus 8:1-2); the plague of gnats, the twenty-seventh day of the sixth month(Exodus 8:16-17); the plague of insects or flies, the twenty-ninth day of the sixth month (Exodus 8:21, 24); the plague on livestock, the second day of the seventh month(Exodus 9:3-6); the plague of boils, the third day of the seventh month (Exodus 9:10); the plague of hail, the fifth day of the seventh month (Exodus 9:22); the plague of locusts, the eighth day of the seventh month (Exodus 10:12-15); the plague of darkness, the tenth day of Abib (Exodus 10:21-23); and the plague of death, on the fifteenth day of Abib (Exodus 11:4, 5).

While there is no definitive proof for these dates, it is reasonable that God would cause the plagues to afflict the Egyptian people in a short span of time to produce the optimum effect and hasten the Pharaoh's decision to allow the Israelites to leave.

The Plague of Blood (Exodus 7:14-18)

Chuck Swindoll says that "God's first punch was a body blow to the heart of Egyptian life" (Swindoll, pg. 176). The mighty Nile was central to the daily life of the Egyptians. It was vital in providing water for everything from washing dishes and cooking to washing one's body while many of the wells were contaminated. In addition to providing for the water needs of the population, it's fish was the primary staple in the national diet. For seven days and nights, the Egyptians had nothing to drink and much of their daily diet was missing as well. Not even the water already stored away in their homes was spared, "blood [was} everywhere in Egypt, even in the wooden buckets and stone jars" (v. 19). The writer of Exodus tells us that the stench from the Nile was so bad that they could not drink its water.

The classical historian, Plutarch, tells us of the importance of the Nile to the Egyptians. When we read in the text that Pharaoh went down into the Nile, it could have been for several reasons: to bathe, perform some religious ablution, or to worship the Nile which was an object of worship to the Egyptians. The degree to which the Egyptian esteem the Nile applied to the quality of the water itself, so much so that it was believed to be compared to ordinary water in quality as champaign is to wine. Egyptians Muslims believed if Mohammed had drunk from the Nile he would have implored God to let him live forever, so that he would never have to be without its continual gratification. Folklore holds that the Turks were so enamored with its water they would eat salt to peak their thirst, and people could easily drink buckets of it in a day without any incontinence. So this river was not only important for its multiple uses in the Egyptian's daily life, it was worshiped and revered. Adam Clarke, in his Bible commentary, writes of the significance of the plague:

> The plague of the bloody waters may be considered as a display of retributive justice against the Egyptians, for the murderous decree which enacted that all the male children of the Israelites should be drowned in that river, the waters of which, so necessary to their support and life, were now rendered not only insalubrious but deadly, by being turned into blood. As it is well known that the Nile was a chief object of Egyptian idolatry, (See Clarke note on "Ex 7:15"|,) and that annually they sacrificed a girl, or as others say, both a boy and a girl, to this river, in gratitude for the benefits received from it, (Universal Hist., vol. i., p. 178, fol. edit.)
>
> God might have designed this plague as a punishment for such cruelty: and the contempt poured upon this object of their adoration, by turning its waters into blood, and rendering them fetid and corrupt, must have had a direct tendency to correct their idolatrous notions, and

lead them to acknowledge the power and authority of the true God.

Interestingly, blood is the elixir of life that courses through the veins of the physical body, even as the Nile was the elixir of life coursing through the body of Egypt. The Egyptian could no more do without the Nile than the body could do with its blood. The Egyptians might have worshiped the Nile, revered it, and boasted of its qualities, but God shows that He is greater and that He can negate all that the Nile represents. Pharaoh is unaffected, however, because his magicians were able to turn water into blood as well. Some ancient manuscripts name these magicians and thereby we discover the origin of Janis and Jambris. They were famous for their power, perhaps derived from familial spirits, and their contention with Moses and Aaron. As powerful as they appeared they were unable, though, to turn the blood back into water and so for a week the Egyptians suffered with no water.

There is nothing in the text to suggest that the Israelites were exempted from the plagues, at least the first three plagues, God sent upon the Egyptians, but it occurs to this writer God would have allowed only the Israelites and not the Israelites to suffer without water, and yet if there were water in Goshen surely the Egyptians would have known about it and collected it. Could it be that the Israelites suffered along with the Egyptians, or was it that God so insulated the Israelites that they never suffered? It is an interesting question for which there is perhaps no answer.

What do you do without water? The water from the wells

was contaminated and rainwater was not an option. The fish are dead and the stench is so foul as to create continual nausea. The hope was that Pharaoh would relent, but God already knew the hardness of his heart and that more than one plague would be needed. So after seven days, Moses returned to Pharaoh to renew his request and again Pharaoh resisted.

The Plague of Frogs (Exodus 8:1-2)

The second exacted upon the Egyptians comes on the heels of the first. Barely is the plague over when Moses returns to Pharaoh and says in effect "if you have had enough then let God's people go, but if not there will be a plague of frogs that will infest your land. Pharaoh's response was certainly predictable, he refused to relent and allow the Israelites to retreat to the wilderness. Therefore, Moses is left with no option but to have Aaron stretch forth the rod of God and call forth frogs from the lakes, streams, ponds, canals, creeks, rivers, any body of water.

Now frogs in and of themselves are not generally considered to be dangerous creatures. They are not particularly frightening, but neither are they particularly enticing unless one views them as s source of food. But taken in vast numbers they would be seen as despicable. Can you imagine what it would be like to awaken in the morning to discover frogs, toads of all shapes, colors, and sizes infiltrating every conceivable crag and cranny? The text tells us that frogs were in the palace, in bedrooms and beds, in ovens and kneading troughs (v. 3). These ovens were a hole in the ground, in which the ancients would insert a kind of earthen pot, which having sufficiently heated, they would stick their cakes inside. Once baked, they would remove them and replace with others, and so on. Imagine heating these ovens in preparation for your daily baking only to discover them filled with frogs. It is almost too grotesque to imagine. There was no place one could step where frogs were not present.

Once again Pharaoh is unimpressed for his magicians are able to do the same thing, but it is not long before Moses and Aaron are called back before him because evidently while able to produce the frogs Janis and Jambris are not able to rid the nation of them. This is where the text gets interesting to the point of being comical. Moses asks the Pharaoh when he would like God to rid the land of the frogs except in the Nile, and Pharaoh says "tomorrow" (v.9). Unbelievable! Pharaoh could have specified any time that he wished, but he says "tomorrow." It is beyond incredible that anyone would desire to exist one moment more than is necessary with the plague of squishy frogs under their feet. Yet Pharaoh is content to live another day, another night with his condition.

Pharaoh here, however, is symbolic of many people that are content to coexist with their negative conditions. I am committed being rid of whatever has me bound. I don't want to spend one more night, not one more minute than is absolutely necessary with whatever stands in my path. But Moses did as the Pharaoh had indicated and the frogs died in the land and were piled up into heaps, "and the land reeked of them" (v.14); a reminder of the arrogance of the Egyptian authorities. It is suggested that it was in these rotting piles of frog carcasses that the flies were birthed reminding us that God never works a miracle where the end of it can be accomplished merely by natural means.

The Plague of Gnats (Exodus 8:16, 17)

The third plague inflicted upon the Egyptian nation was that of gnats. Moses instructs Aaron to "stretch out your staff and strike the dust of the ground and throughout the land of Egypt the dust will become gnats", and it was so. Imagine that every particle of dust in the land become a gnat. I have been exposed to swarms of minute bugs in my life but nothing in my experience could begin to fathom what this must have been like. Surely the sky itself must have become dark by the sheer magnitude of the infestation.

What kind of bug or insect was this? Artapanus, a heathen historian gives this account, "Moses smote the earth with a rod, and produced a certain flying animal, which greatly distressed the Egyptians, and raised ulcers in their bodies, which no physicians could cure." Classical historian, Origen describes this creature as, "having wings and flying in the air, but so subtle and minute as to escape the eye, unless very sharp-sighted; but when it lights upon a body, it stings most bitterly, so that what a man cannot see flying, he feels stinging." Had I been the king I would certainly have broken at this point as a result of the severity of the plague. Every time one opened their mouth to take a breath of air they inhaled a mouthful of insects. One most likely had to shield their eyes to prevent the bugs from flying in and blinding them. It was not a plague with which I would have wanted to contend.

One commentator remarks that manner in which the gnats (or as some translations have it, the lice) appeared was truly miraculous. For lice or gnats, generally, do not come from dust but thrive from the sweat and nastiness of bodies that seem allergic to showers and baths, and that this miracle was like the initial creation of humanity itself that was from the dust of the earth.

It is interesting that this was the first of the three thus far that the king's magicians could not replicate. Instead, the magicians concluded that this plague was the hand of God. What a ringing endorsement for the King of kings and the Lord of lords. Only God could have brought this infestation on the nation and in their opinion, though not specifically stated, only God could deliver them from it. It sounds to me as though there is a pleading in the affirmation for the king to relent that there might be relief from the plague. However, the king's heart would harden all the more and more plagues would come.

The Plague of Flies (Exodus 8:21-24)

The fourth plague to come upon the Egyptians was that of flies. As I suggested in the earlier commentary on the plague of frogs, it is thought that the flies may have germinated in the piles of rotting frogs that cluttered the land. If such a supposition is true then these flies would have carried with them awful diseases that perhaps killed many of the Egyptians.

There is reason, however, to suggest that this plague consisted of more than flies. The Hebrew word used here is generally thought to imply a mixture of many different types of insects and not just flies. So the plague was far worse than that of just pesky flies carrying all manner of sickness and disease, it was swarms of all types of insects and bugs.

This is also the first time that it is explicitly stated that the land of Goshen was exempted from this plague. God now intentionally places a division between His people and the Egyptians so that there are no swarms in Goshen. All of Egypt is infested with flies, all manner of insects, but Goshen is exempted. Clearly, God wants the Egyptian king to know of his love for and protection of the Israelite children. Still, the heart of the king is hardened and he remains steadfast in his resolve to keep the Israelite children enslaved, so the mighty hand of God is forced to send yet another plague upon the Egyptians.

The Plague on Livestock (Exodus 9:3-6)

One would think that the Egyptian king would have learned his lesson with the loss of fish from the daily diet, but now the livestock of the land is targeted. God set a specific time so that there would be no mistaking that it was by anything other than God's hand that the damage had been done. But Pharaoh did not learn his lesson and now the cattle, horses, donkeys, camels, goats, and sheep are affected. First, there was no fish, now there is no red meat. Can you imagine the piles of bloated carcasses littering the landscape? The sheer magnitude of the plague and the odor it had to have emitted certainly made the piles of frogs seem pleasant. But over in Goshen the livestock belonging to the Israelites were not only not affected, they actually flourished. Even the livestock owned by the Pharaoh being tended in Goshen could not escape the plague, but those belonging to the Israelites did.

Reading the text one should see that it is not only the red meat and milk supply that is affected but the transportation as well. The cattle, goats, and sheep provided meat and, in the case of the cattle and the goats, milk. But the camels, horses, and donkey provided much-needed transportation. Who would not pull the chariot of the king? Who would pull the chariots of the warriors? How would people, accustomed to traveling in style, get around? Surely they would not be expected to get out and walk?

It should be evident, by now, that the whole of Egyptian life was being adversely affected by the refusal of the king to honor the request of Moses. One would be forgiven to wonder why someone did not try to overthrow the king and put an end to the madness. Still, Pharaoh refuses to allow the Israelites to leave to go sacrifice. The people are suffering, the economy is affected, but the king is relentless in his resolve to control the situation, somehow he thinks that he is in charge.

It is a risky thing to fancy oneself in charge of their life and that of those within their circle of influence. Many people have been deluded into believing that it is their life and they are free to do with it whatever they desire. The choice to destroy or save one's life is certainly their choice to make, but one must remember that our lives do not belong to us but to God. God is so jealous of what He has put in us when He made us that He says that if we destroy our bodies that He will destroy us. Pharaoh would soon find out how serious God is about those whom He has made, appointed and anointed.

The Plague of Boils (Exodus 9:10)

Met with continued resistance, Moses is instructed to take dust in his hand in the presence of the king and cast it into the air and as it lit on the Egyptians it became boils, or "inflamed eruptions, breaking forth into skin pustules." There is no indication in scripture that the previous plague came to end, God simply calls forth another plague on top of the one already underway. This plague is a particularly nasty plague. Anyone who has had one boil can testify to the agony associated with it, but in this plague boils broke out over the entire body. The magicians that had been showing that they could replicate the miracles that Moses and Aaron wrought are not unable because of the condition they find themselves in. They, like the rest of the nation, are stricken with painful boils over their entire bodies.

It was the custom in ancient times to sit in piles of ash, pouring over one's body when mourning. There is some sense in which when Job is stricken that his sitting in the ash was designed to give him physical relief from the malady that had affected him. So now the thing that often times would bring relief is used to bring affliction. The plague of boils affected everything, human and animal, most certainly even the Pharaoh himself and, still, he is relentless in his opposition to releasing the Israelites to go and offer sacrifice in the wilderness.

The Plague of Hail (Exodus 9:22-28)

The seventh plague is the plague of hail. The announcement of this plague is accompanied by a promise by God to unleash the full force of his plagues against the king, his officials, and his people so that all might know that there is no one like the Lord in all the earth. Reading this account and the promise to unleash the full force of His plagues had me wondering what it was that had been happening to this point. The preceding plagues were terrible in their impact. The country was devastated, the economy ruined and surely the hopes of the people were dashed. God instructs Moses to warn the Egyptians to bring in from the fields their slaves (the slaves mentioned here must have been slaves from other nations since the Israelites were exempted from the plagues) and their livestock, which must have been other than horses, cattle, donkeys, goats, camels, and sheep because they were all dead from the previous plague. It is mind-boggling to me that some people would dare defy the warning, but as their king was defiant and rebellious so also were the people, proving the maxim that maintains that leaders produce after their own kind.

The full force of God's plagues is evidenced in this plague. It was probably not common to see hail in Egypt—after all this was a desert nation. Yet the text maintains that this was the worst storm in the history of Egypt as a nation, "It was the worst storm in all the land of Egypt since it had become a nation" (v. 24b). Accompanied by thunder, the hail landed on everything and everybody destroying in the fields what had not already been destroyed. The only crops not destroyed were the wheat and spelt because it was not their harvesting season. This plague was so devastating that the king's heart finally softened to the point that he admitted that he had sinned against God and asked Moses to stop the plague and he would then let the people go. But as soon as the plague was over the heart of Pharaoh once again hardened and he refused to let the people go, which comes as no surprise to Moses who told Pharaoh that he knew that his mind was not changed and that as soon as the hail and thunder stopped he would change his mind again. Some things never change.

The Plague of Locusts (Exodus 10:12-15)

The eighth plague provides the king of Egypt with yet another opportunity to change his mind and release the Israelite people. The plague promises to send locusts that will "cover the face of the ground so that it cannot be seen. They will devour what little you have left after the hail, including every tree that is growing in your fields. They will fill your houses and those of all your officials and all the Egyptians – something neither fathers nor your forefathers have ever seen from the day the day they settled in this land till now" (vs. 5, 6). The call of Moses for the king to reconsider or experience a plague more terrible than the previous ones is this time reinforced by the king's own advisors and magicians who see their nation devastated and wonder how much more they can take.

It appears that, finally, Pharaoh is willing to listen to reason as he calls Moses and Aaron back into his presence, but it quickly becomes evident that he is still trying to deal with God and God's people on his own terms. The king is willing to release the people but wants to know who it is that will be going. He is willing to allow the men to go but not the women and the children. The king wants to have an insurance policy against a mass exodus. It is amazing to me that after all that has happened that the king still believes that he is in charge. But God is in not the mood to negotiate or to play the king's games, without any more discussion or warning the plague is unleashed; and once again the king summons Moses and Aaron to repent of his stubbornness and again his heart is hardened once the plague is lifted.

The Plague of Darkness (Exodus 10:21-23)

With the ninth plague, one can almost feel the confrontation between Moses and the Egyptian king coming to a dramatic crescendo. As a result of Pharaoh's continued rebellion and his refusal to humble himself before the living God, God causes darkness to cover the land for three days. Everywhere in Egypt there was total darkness except in Goshen where the children of Israel had light. The description of this darkness is interesting, for it was a "darkness that can be felt." I wondered what it meant by "darkness that can be felt." Perhaps, the front that brought the darkness brought also a damp coldness that has a way of chilling one to the bone. Maybe, it was accompanied by a fog so thick it prevented any rays of sun from shinning through. Whatever the cause of the darkness it was one that could be felt and so acute that no one could see anyone else in it or leave their house. So even the lights from torches and fires were not enough to illumine the city.

As before the plague gets the king's attention and he summons Moses and Aaron to implore them to ask God to relent, but again he wants to deal with God on his own terms. Unable to convince Moses to take just the men and leave the women and children the last time, now he attempts to convince him to take everyone but leave the livestock. I am certain that the king has his eyes on the Israelite's flocks and herds since his and the nations' have been depleted by the plagues, but he discovers that Moses can be as insistent and stubborn as he can, which causes him to fly into a rage, harden his heart, refuse to release the Israelites, and ban Moses and Aaron from ever coming into his presence again upon pain of death.

The Plague of Death (Exodus 11:4, 5)

Now comes the grand climax of the ten plagues, the plague of death. The sentence God pronounces upon Egypt is a particularly gruesome plague. "Every firstborn son in Egypt will die, from the firstborn son of Pharaoh, who sits on the throne to the firstborn son of the slave girl, who is at her hand mill, and all the firstborn of the cattle as well" (v.5). But before the plague is released the Israelites are told to ask their Egyptian neighbors for articles of gold and silver, and the Egyptians, whom the Lord had made "favorably disposed" toward them and Moses, gave them everything for which they asked. Never in their wildest dreams could the Egyptians have imagined what was getting ready to happen as a result of the stubborn refusals of their king. The text tells us that this plague was so severe that it brought a loud wailing throughout Egypt that was worse than it had ever been before or would be. Only those whose houses, lentels, and doorposts had been painted with the blood of the lamb would be spared as the death angel passed over.

This tenth and final plague would be "the straw that broke the camel's back." Confronted with the grief of losing his first born son the Egyptian king finally relents and allows the Israelites to depart. After 430 years to the day that a large family entered Egypt, a small nation leaves carrying the articles of clothing, silver, and gold for which they had been instructed to ask from their Egyptian masters. There are some interesting and natural leadership principles we can glean from tis account.

Principle One: *There is no obstacle too great for God.*

Jesus declares, "The things that are impossible with people are possible with God" (Luke 18:27). We, humans, are frail and limited. There are many things that are beyond our ability. In contrast, however, there is nothing too difficult for our God. Our natural inclination is to rely upon our own ability, knowledge, and authority and when we reach our limit believe that all is lost. Once a king came to power in Egypt that cared nothing for the legacy of Joseph and the promises that had been made to him Israel's long nightmare began. For 430 years the Israelites endured the hardship of enslavement. As the days, months and years slowly slipped by and generation after generation disappeared any resistance must have surely given way to resignation as they slowly lost hope and accepted their fate. So when Moses showed up announcing the Lord's concern for them one can imagine an excitement and anticipation that was probably guarded. Then suddenly their initial excitement is shattered as the Egyptian responds to Moses' demands by forcing them to maintain their daily quota of bricks but takes away their straw. Their hopes shattered and their fears confirmed they turn on Moses and Aaron. One can almost hear them saying, "I told you so!"

Their deliverance did not happen overnight. In the long scheme of things, considering the length of their captivity, time appeared passed quickly, but when one is in trouble time seems to stand still. The plagues dramatically demonstrate that God is God and there is no one beside Him. He is not limited by that which limits us. There is nothing He cannot do. There is no obstacle by which He can be contained or that He cannot overcome. The amount of time it takes does not matter, nor the length of time one must wait until the fulfillment of their expectation. None of that can ever invalidate the promises, intentions, or plans God has for His people. Those things that seem insurmountable are nothing but obstacles to be overcome to God.

Principle Two: *A hardened heart will cause you great pain.*

Every time God sent another plague on Egypt He would also turn and harden the king's heart so that the things the king promised he would do would not get done. It is rather like the believer that finding him or herself in trouble seeks the Lord for deliverance, but once the deliverance has come returns to their former way of strife. It seems unreasonable that someone, anyone, would play such foolish games with God, but people do it every day. People who are in power, who sit in seats of authority, who exert a level of control over their environment do not like to be out of control. They do not like encountering anything that defies their ability, because they are extremely confident in them. Such confidence is desirable but can lead to a heart that is 'hardened.'

In this account, the pain that emanated from the king's hardened heart was too much for him to bear. His own firstborn son, and not just those of his subjects, was killed. The king of Egypt was worshiped as a god. He was to be above such calamity. His magicians and sorcerers could not undo this feat, nor could it be minimalized in any way. The king gave in and the Israelites were not simply released, but expelled from their 430-year enslavement, "Because of my mighty hand he will let them go; because of my mighty hand he will drive them out of his country" (Exodus 6:1). It was quite a price to pay for arrogantly and stubbornly holding on, refusing to acknowledge the power and sovereignty of the One true and living God.

We are not so different from this Egyptian king, are we? Time without number we, too, have allowed our hearts to become hard and callous toward the instructions and directives, the commandments and ordinances of God. We like to blame outside factors for our pain and want to be certain they have some significant impact. Yet, the biggest factor is our own stubborn self-will. In another time when corporal punishment in the home was not so nearly frowned upon as it is today, a common expression was, "a hard head makes for a sore behind." We can get what we desire, even if it is out of God's will for our lives, but we will surely suffer the consequences for the decisions we make and the actions we take; and, then we discover that 'a hardened heart will cause you great pain.'

Principle Three: *God will not take no for an answer.*

Repeatedly Moses went to the king and announced that the great God of Heaven said, "let my people go!" It was an announcement the king could not hear, would not hear, stubbornly refused to hear. In his mind he was god, the Israelites were his people, and he was not going to be told what to do by anybody. From the first audience with the king, it was clear that any overture from Moses was going to be met with great resistance. The Egyptian king retaliated swiftly, first demanding the Israelites collect their own straw, then taking it away altogether while still demanding that the daily quota of bricks be met. In most instances, such a rejection would be sufficient to put a stop to future overtures, and in this instance quitting was nearly what Moses was inclined to do. "O Lord, why have you brought trouble on this people? Is this why you sent me? Ever since I went to Pharaoh to speak in your name, he has brought trouble upon this people, and you have not rescued your people at all."

Moses' tirade sounds like many of my own, and mine were no more successful than his. God had determined to intervene in the affairs of his people. He had determined that their misery and suffering because of their masters was enough. Their cries had reached Him and now they were to be given relief by being freed and set into a "good and spacious land, a land flowing with milk and honey" (Exodus 3:8). Clearly, God was not in the mood to take 'no' for an answer. In fact, the king's resistance was anticipated, even necessary. It was not just the king that needed to know that God was faithful to His Word to see that it is fulfilled (Jeremiah 1:12), the Israelites needed to know it more. Just as Moses expected that the king would relent at the first announcement, the people did as well and when it did not happen and the king retaliated the people took their frustration out on Moses, "May the Lord look upon you and judge you! You have made us a stench to Pharaoh and his officials and have put a sword in his hands to kill us" (Exodus 5:21).

For 430 years the Israelites had lived in captivity under the influence of Egyptian worship and culture. For 430 years they had not heard from the God of their fathers in the manner that Abraham, Isaac, and Jacob had heard. Their faith needed to be built. They needed to be prepared for the arduous journey of nation-building that was yet to come. Every bit of resistance, every plague was necessary to get the people from where they had been for all these years to where their God wanted them to be. God could not say 'no,' He would not say 'no!' It was necessary that He persist so the Israelites could see His faithfulness. Is it a possibility that those things in our lives we have not caused and that seem to persist are intended by God to move us from where we have been to where He wants us to be? If so, then rest assured that He will not take 'no' for an answer.

Principle Four: *When God is for you none can be against you.*

For 430 years Israel had been enslaved, mercilessly and cruelly terrorized and brutalized. Their suffering was so great that they had resigned themselves to accepting it as their lot. The king was seen as omnipotent and seemingly no one could stand against him. This belief was confirmed by the number of times the king would agree to release them from their captivity only to change his mind. The magicians and enchanters replicated many of the miracles Moses performed solidifying the belief that none could stand against Egypt's Pharaoh. In the natural none could stand against the power and might of the Egyptian king. In the natural he was omnipotent. Who then would dare oppose him?

God had heard the cries of the Israelites at the severity of their suffering and was set to rescue them and bring them out of Egypt and into the promised land (Exodus 3:7-8). One could well wonder why it took 430 years for God to act, but Israel was not yet a nation when they entered the land of Goshen. They were only a small family living in the afterglow of Joseph's favor, but soon a new king would come to power that knew nothing about Joseph, who saw the potential both for abuse and economic gain. "Now a new king arose over Egypt, who did not know Joseph. He said to his people, "Behold, the people of the sons of Israel are more and mightier than we. 'Come, let us deal wisely with them, or else they will multiply and in the event of war, they will also join themselves to those who hate us, and fight against us and depart from the land.' So they appointed taskmasters over them to afflict them with hard labor. And they built for Pharaoh storage cities, Pithom and Raamses" (Exodus 1:8-11). The Egyptian king's purposes were nationalistic and reactive. Here were these immigrants living in the best of the land and growing at such an alarming rate that by sheer numbers they could soon outnumber the Egyptians themselves. Here was an opportunity to both check their growth and at the same time compel laborers to build their cities. But God's plan and intention were different.

Is it possible that God was allowing the Israelites to suffer in order to build a nation forged through hardship and not opulence? Is it possible that God knew this large family could not achieve the nation status for which they were destined, according to the promise first given to Abraham, until they increased in number and strength of character? A generation is about 35 to 40 years, so at least eight to ten generations had endured hardship and suffering under the cruel hand of the taskmasters. But they had also developed all types of trades and skills that would be necessary once they reached the Promised

Land. Now all that remained was the arduous task of changing a generational mindset of enslavement. Israel lacked hope and courage. Who were they compared to the might of Egypt? "What then shall we say to these things? If God *is* for us, who *is* against us" (Romans 8:31)?

We are often faced with seemingly insurmountable odds. The task of leading a people where God intends can often seem impossible. There are times when people will seem more content continuing to live under the cruelty of the suffering they have known and are accustomed to rather than venture forth into the unknown. Like the Israelites, what they lack is hope. Yet, the plagues tangibly demonstration that the power and might of the Egyptian king could not compare to the power and might of their God. It might often appear that God does not care or is, at least, dispassionately interested in what happens to His people. But, God plans to do His people good and not harm. He knows everything about our circumstances and is at work in the midst of them to accomplish His purposes.

We have a luxury the Israelites did not. We have a record of the faithfulness of our God. Just as nothing could stand in the path of God when He determined to end the Israelite's suffering and bring them out into a land flowing with milk and honey, nothing can stand in the path of what God has determined to do in our lives and ministries. "Know that the LORD Himself is God; It is He who has made us, and not we ourselves; *We are* His people and the sheep of His pasture" (Psalm 100:3). That we are His own people should fill us with joy and confidence that no one can be against us.

Conclusion

It occurs to me that many trying to serve God's people are more like Moses than they dare to openly admit. We all struggle with validating our vocation, thinking that God would be far, far better off choosing someone else. After all, there are many who possess greater gifts than we could ever imagine having ourselves, and yet, God chose us. Is it not interesting how some things come easier to others than they come to us, how it appears that we have to work harder and longer than others and still our final product seems inferior in comparison? Whether our perception is correct or not is not nearly as important as the fact that part of our struggle lies in our estimation of ourselves. Rather than walking confidently in what we know about ourselves to be true, we judge ourselves using a measuring rod intended for someone else. When God called us He knew precisely what He was getting. He knew not only what we could do, but also what we were capable of doing under and in the right circumstances.

We may not have ever openly challenged God in the manner Moses did, when he encountered Him on the backside of the wilderness near a bush that burned but was not consumed; however, we may have never stepped out in faith to do the seemingly impossible because we had already determined that we were not the right one to do it and that we would fail. Some have said that it was Benjamin Franklin that once said, "Nothing ventured, nothing gained." Whether this attribution is correct or not, what is true is that if one refuses to risk, they will never find reward. Failure is in refusing to go on, not in being blocked from going on. God has richly endowed us with gifts and abilities far beyond our comprehension. Just as there are things that are challenging for us, there are also things that come without challenge. This book was not so much concerned with those things that do not challenge us as it was with those things that do. If God has called us then our responsibility is to confidently and affirmatively respond to that call by walking in obedience to it. This book has been dedicated to that end.

I started this book listing the six characteristics, which many secular writers have previously asserted, effective leadership requires: honesty and integrity, outstanding self-awareness, vision, courage, communication skills, and team building. Each of these characteristics is valid and important, but when addressing the particularities of spiritual leadership in the church, I added unflinching obedience to God, correct timing, clear communication, and a willingness to share the burden of leadership with others. I have attempted to demonstrate in this book how these four additional characteristics, more specific to the household of faith, were operative in the life of Moses; and, by, extension should be operative in the life of the leader if she/he is to be effective.

I wish I could state with assurance that I have arrived at a place where my leadership has been perfected to a level viewed as effective. But in some senses, 'effective' is in the eye of the beholder, and if this assertion is true then effective leadership will be different depending on the leader(s) and community where leadership is being exercised and is best evaluated. As for me, my story is still in the process of being written. I know what it is like to lead in Egypt. I know what it is like to lead in the wilderness. I know what it is like to lead in the Promised Land. I also know what it is like to seemingly take two steps backwards while progressing forward only one. It is in these instances where a proper understanding of the principles I have attempted to lift out of the life of Moses in Egypt will become increasingly important.

Moses had his challenges, but he also had his God with him. He endured much in his confrontations with the king of Egypt and he was victorious. What he did not know, however, was that those confrontations and challenges were the prelude to greater ones yet to come. I join with those who would love to believe that overcoming a challenge ensured continual victory, but the sad truth is that challenge leads to greater challenge. Overcoming the challenge does not insulate us from encountering more, but it does embolden us and prepare us for what is yet to come. Leaders will encounter and be stretched by challenges that come one right after the other. It will feel at times that the job of a leader is to constantly extinguish fires, and one could argue that putting out fires is part of the job description. The key to effectively confronting them lies in how we approach them.

We will see how Moses handled these challenges in the next volume. There the seed of Abraham, now a small nation of desert babies, must learn how to live free. It is a new challenge for them and for their leader. Their odyssey often highlighted the expression, "you can take them out of Egypt, but you cannot get Egypt out of them." Moses would encounter rebellion, challenges to his leadership from his own family, grumbling, mumbling and complaining that was so intense at times that Moses would ask God to kill them, but at other times he would intervene and intercede for the people when God had enough.

Some reading this may say I am painting a depressing picture, and I understand because it takes a special person to lead the people of God. Moses will try to do it on his own, ignoring the fourth characteristic of effective spiritual leadership: a willingness to share the burden of leadership with others, but soon discover that he cannot. We will see in the wilderness where he can no longer ignore this characteristic and must make an adjustment, but adjustments and the willingness, perhaps the foresight, to make them, too, is a characteristic of effective leadership.

When I began my pastoral ministry nearly four decades ago, I had no idea what I was getting myself into. My professional training had not adequately prepared me for the challenges I getting ready to face. My romanticized view blinded me to how difficult and challenging ministry could be.

There were times when, like Moses, I asked God to get me out of what I was in and where I was serving. There were other times that I made allowances for the people and pled their case before the Lord. There were times when I thought I could please everybody until I discovered that goal was misplaced. But I was pliable, teachable. I soaked up everything I could. I sought out seasoned spiritual giants who could give me insight and, mostly, became comfortable with failing only to get up and start again.

Moses was not a perfect leader, though he was the leader Israel needed. We will never be perfect leaders, but let us rest in the assurance that we were and are the leaders the people needed and that God required and was pleased to use for the moment. Let us also rest in the assurance that though we are not perfect, we are pliable, willing to be transformed into the leader He has anointed us and appointed us to be. It is to that end I continue to serve and lead.

Moses

About The Author

Dr. James H Logan, Jr. is the Founder of Jim Logan Evangelistic Ministry and Kingdom Fellowship of Churches, Co-Founder and Senior Pastor of Kingdom Fellowship Christian Center, and Head of the Department of Urban Christian Studies at Charlotte Christian College and Theological Seminary in Charlotte, North Carolina.

Dr. Logan completed his secondary education at Williston-Northampton School in Easthampton, MA; received his Bachelor of Arts Degree from Kenyon College in Gambier, Ohio; his Master of Divinity Degree from Princeton Theological Seminary in Princeton in Princeton, New Jersey; and, his Doctor of Ministry Degree from Columbia Theological Seminary in Decatur, Georgia. He is working to complete a Ph.D. in theology from William Seymour College in Washington DC.

A former member of the Board of Trustees of Princeton Theological Seminary, Dr. Logan presently serves on the Board of Advisors and as an Adjunct Professor of Urban Ministry for Gordon Conwell Theological Seminary-Charlotte, North Carolina. He presently serves as professor and Head of the Department of Urban Christian Studies at Charlotte Christian College and Theological Seminary, also in Charlotte, NC.

Dr. Logan is best known for his renewal ministry of powerful preaching and teaching in congregations and conferences throughout the Church, across the country, and internationally including in The Democratic Republic of the Congo and Nigeria, as well as Brussels, Belgium.

James and his wife, Sybil, have three children and five grandchildren and reside in Charlotte, North Carolina.

Moses

Moses

Bibliography

Clarke, Adam. *Commentary on the Whole Bible* Nashville, TN: Thomas Nelson Incorporated, 1997

Getz. Gene. *Freeing Yourself to Know God.* Nashville, TN: Broadman & Holman, 1997.

Swindoll, Charles, *Moses: A Man of Selfless Dedication.* W. Publishing Group: 1999.

Alexander Fraser Tytler, *Universal History of the World: Volume 1 - From the Creation of the World to the Beginning of the Eighteenth Century* London: Forgotten Books, 2018.

www.ingramcontent.com/pod-product-compliance
Lightning Source LLC
Chambersburg PA
CBHW031137090426
42738CB00008B/1121